Cakewalk

Cakewalk

ADVENTURES IN SUGAR WITH MARGARET BRAUN

Text and illustrations by Margaret Braun

Photography by Quentin Bacon

RIZZOLI
NEW YORK

First published in the United States of America in 2001 by
RIZZOLI INTERNATIONAL PUBLICATIONS, INC.
300 Park Avenue South
New York, NY 10010

ISBN: 0-8478-2334-2
LC: 2001086154

Distributed by St. Martin's Press

Manufactured in China

For my parents, Richard and Doris Braun

Acknowledgments

This adventure reflects an extraordinary period of my life that was exciting, challenging, and fueled by the enthusiasm and support of my dear friends, loving family, and valued colleagues. How lucky I am to have such smart and diversely talented people in my life.

Thank you, Liz Sullivan, my visionary and trustworthy editor for getting it, for always being right, and for allowing me the freedom that was so important to me, yet all the while holding this project together with a firm hand. You're the best there is. To Lynne Yeamans, an exceptional designer—thank you for welcoming me into your studio for this unusual collaboration. With style and grace, you made a complicated project into a beautiful book. To Quentin Bacon, thank you for your exquisite photography and calming devotion to this venture—it was inspiring. I love working with you. To Tina Rupp, thank you for your good eye and those gorgeous end pages. You're a dream. To brilliant John Branch, thank you for being meticulous, sitting down with me, and asking all those great questions. I was lucky to work with you. To Kate Krader, thanks for being right there with your food savvy and for setting a twinkling tiara on the entire project. To Signe Bergstrom, thank you for your reliably smart, compact answers. To Rick Spinell, thank you for kneading the breadth of your many talents into the testing of the recipes, and to Marcey Brownstein, for the delicious flavors that come from your kitchen.

Thank you, Michael Grand, for your unequaled generosity and years of gorgeous images, and to Rick Hemmings, for your kindness and artful printing of the photographs. To Amye Dyer, my persevering agent, thank you for helping me finish the proposal, for setting everything up, and introducing me to Liz. I'm grateful to David DelGaizo for providing me access to the mortal coil of this book.

Thank you Dana Cowin, for your genuine enthusiasm and for lighting the spark that resulted in that glorious cakewalk through Barcelona, and to Tina Ujlaki, for your kind words and encouragement over the years and for asking "Where would you like to go?" To Michael and Arianne Batterberry at *Food Arts*, I am sincerely grateful for your support of my work over the years. To Christian Holthausen, thank you for your insightful translation. To Danielle DeVoe, Carrie Pillar, Luciano Vismara, Susan Lantzius, Joe Lanciani, Cheryl Kleinman, Karen Salmansohn, Nancy Arner, Eve Applebaum, Lee Hunt, David Seeley, Barbara Arvanitis, Mary Prlain, Lori Fortunato, Jim Rooney, Ivy Ozer, Jamie James, Paul Elie, James Lyons, Nick Malgieri, and Donna Ferrari, thank you for your involvement across the years.

And warm blanket thanks go to those near and dear to me: to Bernie Katz, Beth Reisman, Lenora Todaro, Terry Savage, Beatrice Braun, and to my brother, Joe Braun, for deeply enriching my life, and to my dear friend Leslie Siegel, whose voice is evident in this work. To my darling Richard Cohen, thank you for your wisdom, humor, and imagination, and for answering all of my questions at the end of the day.

To make a paste of sugre, wherof a man maye make all manner of fruites, and other fyne

thynges, with theyr forme, as platters, dishes, glasses, cuppes, and such like thinges,

wherwith you may furnish a table: and. . . [a]t the end of the Banquet, eate them up. For this

paste is very delicate and savorous. . . A pleasant thing for them that sit at the table.

—Master Alexis of Piedmont, *Secretes* (1558)

Contents

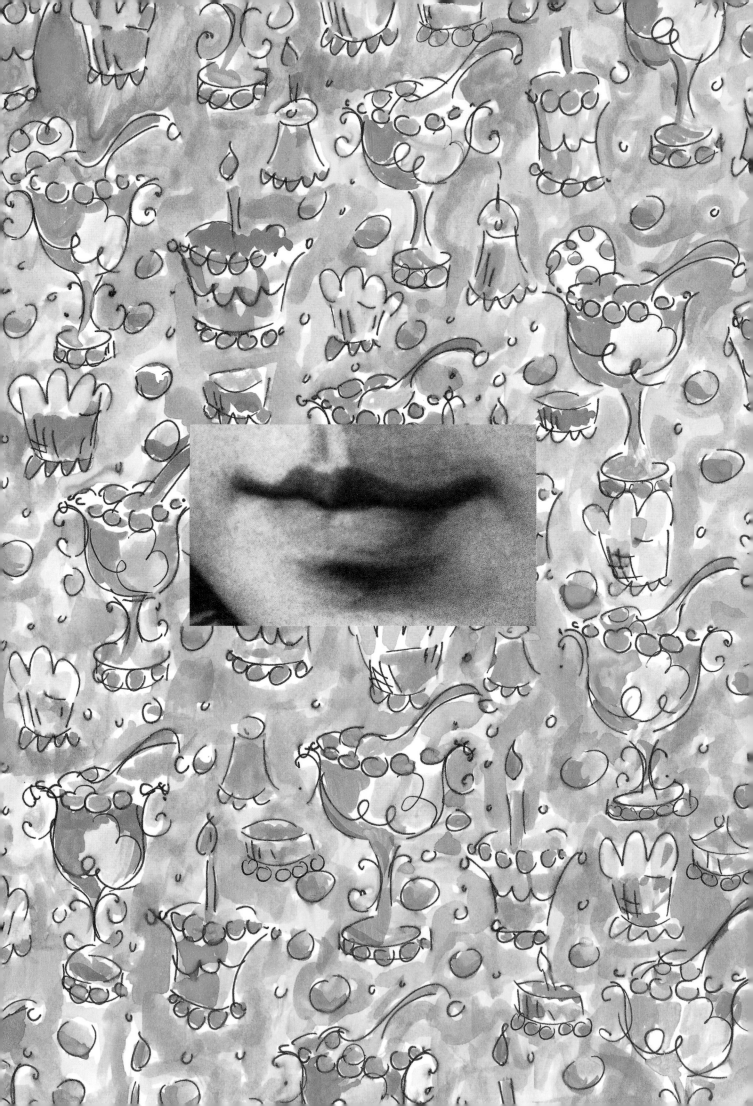

INTRODUCTION

Beauty Is in the Mouth of the Beholder

Taste . . . that of the tongue and the palate . . . is a ready and unreflective discernment, sensitive and sensual in appreciating the good—violent in rejecting the bad, not even knowing if it should be pleased by what is presented to it . . . Taste is not content with seeing, with knowing the beauty of a work; it has to feel it, to be touched by it.

—Voltaire, "Goût," *Encyclopédie* (1751–77)

When I see something beautiful, I want to eat it. This happens to me in museums. A medieval sculpture, a Flemish painting, a Byzantine necklace, and I'm off to the cafeteria. It's not enough to see it. I want to consume it, overcome it. At other times, plagued with love and envy for the person who made it, along with a profound wish to go back in time, I try to stay in the gallery until the hunger gives way to a good idea. Then I'll go back to my studio and try to do something about it. Since I work best on an empty stomach, I might make something beautiful—something that will taste as good as it looks.

Imagine a table decked with delectable sweetmeats: a plate of drunken figs, a soufflé heaving a dark chocolate sigh, spiced kumquats and toasted hazelnuts swimming in pomegranate juice, caramels and baked crèmes, lattice-crusted pastries, and in the center, a tiered cake, festooned with sugar-work swags, intricate piping, gilded in edible gold, and topped by a sugar-paste chalice overflowing with marzipan fruits.

The presentation is mouthwatering. Eager to sink your spoons into it, you hope the flavors will live up to the enticing spectacle, but the judgment awaits the mouth's verdict. The eye evaluates the beauty of the dish, the nose discerns the aroma. Slurps, crunches, and swallows resound inside your head, along with the desire to reach out and touch. Together, sight, smell, sound, and touch determine taste.

This sensory process only applies to the edible arts, which is why good-looking sweetmeats are so pleasurable. Great works of art may whet the appetite but you can't eat them, whereas pretty cakes implore you to. So, making an edible work while I'm energized by a glorious afternoon at the museum brings me that much closer to fulfilling a need to taste that which I love.

How can I stand to work so hard on a cake only to have it taken away, cut into pieces, and devoured? Just knowing there's a chance that the beholder will eat my cake and conclude that it *is* as good as it looks gives me a vicarious thrill, making it all worthwhile.

However, I don't mind if my sugar sculpture is contemplated or admired, and isn't ever consumed, as was the case with the magnificent sugar works by the nineteenth-century confectioner Antonin Careme, who was "anxious to create several large centerpieces that could be preserved for a good number of years."

Don't destroy these sugary marvels,/Prepared to charm your eyes alone:
Or at least wait a few days, in order to grant/These sweet monuments a few days' respite.

—J. De Berchoux, excerpt from "Dessert," *Song IV of La Gastronomie* (1876)

Personal Taste

A cakewalk is a promenade or march in which the person who performs the sassiest, most intricate steps receives a prize, which is cake. A cakewalk, for me, is an inquisitive journey into the essence of a particular time, place, or object in search of its defining characteristics. The prize—the result of the journey—is the making of a cake, which tells its story in sugar, marzipan, icing, and vibrant color, finished with sugar pearls and gold dust.

I was born in Levittown, New York, to a family of musicians and artists and strong opinions: a family obsessed with strong flavors. My mother and father cooked dinner together every night (and still do). They made blood-rare meats, dignified gravies, and hills of Yorkshire pudding. For Thanksgiving, we feasted on capon, stuffed with wild rice, toasty mushrooms, and sharp little bursts of sweet currant, with a side of wine-braised "Mama Baby Onions" (pearl onions squashed with a fork that "give birth" to the little onions inside). We finished dinner with chilled Kirby cucumbers and tomatoes—skinned, seeded, and salted—on a bed of crunchy iceberg lettuce. Noodles and tomatoes (our fast-food favorite) were made with Mueller's egg noodles, a can of plum tomatoes, salt, and about a pound of butter. As for holiday cooking, we boarded the secular bandwagon when the menu sounded good. At Passover, the Charoseth was doctored up with brown sugar, vanilla, and a touch of red wine, making it good enough to throw into a pie shell and bake in the oven. On St. Patrick's Day, a salty, pink corned beef suffered the wrath of the pressure cooker—an ominous fate for a hunk of meat. It was mellowed with sweet potato baked crispy on top, or butter-steamed fresh peas bubbling and spinning under lettuce-leaf blankets. The process: Open the pod, three peas in the mouth, the rest in the pot. The pea shucking took forever and it reaped a wee harvest.

In winter, while the oil burner roared, my mother and I ate pistachio nuts on the warm floor. Green and brown smells snaked up from beneath the kitchen sink—which was home to a self-nourishing ecosystem of shallots, onions, garlic, and potatoes. Above the sink, in avocado stainless steel cabinets, were Hershey bars, licorice nibs, Jujubees, Hydrox cookies, Mallowmars, Cream of Wheat, brown sugar, and soy sauce. A wishbone from last night's chicken hung to dry from the kitchen lamp, which was a white ceramic orb with holes in it—a big round Swiss cheese lit from within. Plump raspberries, the furry, dusty kind, grew beneath the privet hedges in the backyards of our neighborhood. We picked them in our bare feet, drowned them in heavy cream and sugar, and ate them for lunch. In those days, there were still working farms in the middle of the suburbs—remnants of prewar Long Island. During corn season, we'd go to Van Sise Farm to visit the rabbits, the lobsters, and the cider mill, then rustle through the corn bin, peel back all ears, and pick out the ones with the whitest kernels. On the way back, we'd pick up a chicken at the poultry farm in Bethpage. Market availability (local produce, and the seasonal best offered by our local grocer, fishmonger, butcher, or baker) still meant something. But a trip to the supermarket was equally exciting.

My first cakewalks were with my brother, Joe, in Astoria, Queens, where we'd visit our grandmother. She lived on the corner of Crescent Street and she baked Almond Crescents from a recipe in *The Settlement Cookbook*; they crumbled all over our shirts. (My own version includes dried cherries and pistachio nuts, and a bit more butter; see recipe on page 205.)

There is an aroma distinctive to an apartment building hallway when the dinner is cooking in all eighteen apartments at once. And to those of us who grew up in a house instead of an apartment, this aroma was genuinely exotic. Spinning from door to door, we'd take in the warm smells, sweet smells, spicy smells, baked smells, winey smells, vulgar smells of smoked fish, coffee, curry, and potted meats—other-world smells, secret and alarming—until we were dizzy. Then we'd play in the elevator and sneak off to buy *Kourambiethes* (powder cookies) from the Greek bakery under the El.

By 1968, my father—the first American in Levittown to master the art of the wok—was on to sukiyaki and sushi. Too young for chopsticks, my brother and I abandoned our forks and ate with our fingers. Dad had discovered a Japanese grocery in Jamaica, Queens, and he pacified our little mouths with *Botan*—chewy millet-paste candies wrapped in rice paper—which melted on our tongues.

Music played in the foreground, and our relationship to it, like our relationship to food, was democratic yet highly opinionated. Accompanying the music was a soundtrack of crackling bits in oil, the whiny eggbeater, pots crashing, steam escaping from beneath a lid, the faucet, and the dishwasher. Above the music there were the discussions about the music (and sometimes there were serious arguments over who burnt the rice). My father and brother are musicians and they spoke through music; if Joe detected a suspended fourth, my father would put down his pot holder and go into the living room and confirm it on the piano, and we'd all delight in his confirmation of it. Our kitchen song is the tune of dinner in the making, conversation, and music—the mother of the arts. I always listen to music while I work.

It has taken me many meals away from my parents' kitchen to appreciate the beauty of a can of rendered duck fat in the refrigerator door. It's revolting to look at, but it's great for pan-frying potatoes, or as a light *schmear* on rye bread with Kosher salt. A can of duck fat is just a good thing to have around.

Today, if we're all together on a Sunday morning, my mother goes into the china cabinet and hauls out a big old cardboard box, which is lined with contact paper (a geometric pattern in orange, brown, black, and chrome). From the box she pulls out the frayed-edge, grease-stained Sunday Pancake recipe, which she derived from Craig Claiborne's "Pancake Nonpareil" in the *New York Times* (see recipe on page 204). It's basically Yorkshire pudding without the beef fat, plus more butter and egg, and pools of fresh lemon juice sprinkled with insurmountable helpings of confectioners' sugar. Doubling the recipe makes two 12-inch skillets' worth, and is never enough. She also makes a Flourless Chocolate Yule Log (see recipe on page 203) filled with fresh unsweetened whipped cream and dusted with bitter cocoa. I am still trying to convince her that the way her Yule log cracks when she rolls it up is a good thing—that the flawless spiral of a Yodel or a HoHo may be a theoretical improvement, but not to be compared with the home-made original. My father can still be found at the stove modifying his fudge recipe at three in the morning. He is also the spaetzle king. I have to say that though my parents put loving care into serving us extraordinary meals, it was never about overabundance—we never stuffed ourselves sick, and there was always room for dessert.

Why did I become a sugar artist? I always wanted to be an artist. But I never intended to work with food—it just happened that way. Having absorbed the peculiar wisdom of a family living in a gastronomical bubble left me feeling right at home in the kitchen. So working in a kitchen seemed the logical next step.

I was twenty years old, and it was time to move on. But how was I to support myself? By 1982 my résumé read as follows:

1978—Short-order waitress/egg slinger at Greek diner

1978—Melon baller for dawning of '70s salad-bar frenzy

1979—Tabbouleh maker during height of health food craze

1980—Veal sausage maker at ravioli shop

1981—Quiche maker at gourmet shop

1982—Cannoli filler at Italian-American bakery

My father gave me some career advice. He said, "Pick a street, and walk into every bakery on that street and say this: 'I am looking for a job.'" I had decorated a cake once. It was a white fluffy thing with strawberry goo leaking from the sides. I think it was a rectangle.

Sant Ambroeus 1983

I landed a job at Sant Ambroeus in New York, a swank Upper East Side Milanese pasticceria. Now, with this job, I had legitimate reasons for eating lots of cake first thing in the morning. The job was demanding. I worked six days a week from 6 A.M. to sundown. However, the long days in a hot kitchen included Italian-style lunch breaks: one hour to eat followed by a stroll through Central Park and a game of Frisbee in our chef whites.

A year later, I took my first paid vacation. Clueless but curious, I chose Italy. I arrived in Milan, where I boarded a bus from the airport that let me off right in front of the largest Gothic cathedral in the world—the magnificent Duomo (1386–1834), the jewel of Milan, graced by the *La Bella Madonina* ("the Beautiful Little Madonna") perched high above piles of stalagmitic spires, offering comfort to outsiders

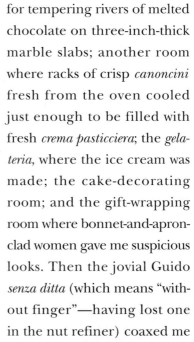

like me. About four blocks northeast of the Piazza Del Duomo is Sant Ambroeus Milano—the older sister shop to Sant Ambroeus in New York. It was early morning and the dining room was already filled with tea-sipping ladies in furs. I can still hear the clink of their porcelain cups. I introduced myself to the maitre d', who let me slip through a secret doorway and make my descent into the belly of the bakery. Luciano, the head baker, greeted me with kisses and we began a dizzying tour of this ancient labyrinth of sugar. First, a room just cool enough for tempering rivers of melted chocolate on three-inch-thick marble slabs; another room where racks of crisp *canoncini* fresh from the oven cooled just enough to be filled with fresh *crema pasticciera*; the *gelateria*, where the ice cream was made; the cake-decorating room; and the gift-wrapping room where bonnet-and-apron-clad women gave me suspicious looks. Then the jovial Guido *senza ditta* (which means "without finger"—having lost one in the nut refiner) coaxed me into scooping a pinkie's worth of warm marzipan from the mixer. All this within my first three hours in a foreign country left me woozy and elated. So began my first cakewalk abroad. I spent the remainder of that day wandering about Milan, being astonished by Leonardo's *Last Supper*, a real-life Baroque palace, and the cruciform ceiling of the Galleria. Then my eyes would fall to street level, and I'd be captivated by the utterly mundane packaging of a box of nails in the window of a hardware store. I returned to New York inspired, and anxious to decorate cakes.

My first cakewalk also calls to mind an over-stuffed backpack, bad shoes, a Eurail pass, too many travel books, an introduction to bottled water, good bread, real tomatoes, odd but friendly encounters encouraged by midday wine-drinking on trains, my first Walkman, and the disorienting, meandering, and marvelous walks through hill towns, medieval villages, and extremely stylish cities. I'm pretty much the same girl today as I was back then except I travel lighter. Over the years, my love for music, the arts, travel, and all things sweet have added dimension to my kitchen song. They have worked their way into my cakes and sugar sculptures.

In the name of taste, and in deference to the eyes,
the art must play on measured spaces and sweet harmonies.

—Jean-Claude Bonnet, *Carême,*
or the Last Sparks of Decorative Cuisine (1977)

A finished cake is like a musical score. When I see a cake bare of decoration, I think about how a composer might feel when seeing a musical staff bare of notation. The written language of music is a codified system of symbols that represent the work. The musical staff is marked with an arrangement of notes per measure, symbolizing the rhythm, melody, and basic structure of a musical work. Like a musical staff, a well-designed cake includes similar components within a comparable structure. For instance; a shell or pearl border or a sequence of evenly placed swags imply the rhythm, while decorations or "decorative notes" like polka dots, fleurs-de-lis, or delicate piping suggest a melody. Added notation to a musical score like phrasing and particular chords, or a crescendo, add color and flavor to the work, while harmonics pick up the light. These characteristics reveal the unmistakable voice of the composer. Just as certain flourishes add rhythm and melody to a cake, features such as color, marzipan fruits, sugar-work tassels, a sugar chalice topper, with harmonics reverberating in gold leaf, denote the personal signature of the cake decorator. A musical score is a silent construction on a sheet of paper in black and white of a musical composition—a topographical map of sorts, with the sounds of the instruments, strings, woodwinds, brass, electric guitar, percussion, and vocals all right there in front of you. Just as some musicians can hear an entire symphony in their heads just by reading the score, I see my finished cakes as compositions, which I can hear inside my head and which I hope play with perfect balance and harmony.

A well-designed cake is also like a well-designed building. A series of tiers are set in place with a solid support system of flat planes and reinforcing beams. Cake decorating at its best combines aspects of music as well as the decorative aspects of architecture. I think of it as a small-scale application of nonfunctional architecture. For example, look at the vaulted arches of a cloister, or a cathedral nave (the central isle of a church extending from the entrance to the apse), then notice the classic swag motif on a cake. There's a likeness, but it's hard to put your finger on. If you turn this book upside down, you'll see how the swags on my cakes are "archlike."

It seems to me that architects have been turning their blueprints upside down for centuries. Just look for the cakelike swag relief pattern on building façades everywhere. But buildings don't look like cakes—cakes look like buildings. Therein lies an interesting correlation between cake decoration and architecture, and I have feelings about that.

To the aid of the dessert call in all the arts,

Especially the one that shines in the Lombard quarter.

There, you're certain to find, to your heart's content,

Sweets arranged into gay buildings,

Castles made of bonbons, biscuit palaces,

The Louvre, Bagatelle and Versailles preserved;

The loves of Sappho, Abelard and Tibullus,

Camacho's wedding and the labors of Hercules,

And a thousand other things that are imitated

By clever sweetmeat makers I could mention by name.

—J. De Berchoux, Excerpt from "Dessert,"

Song IV of La Gastronomie (1876)

I don't like to make cakes as replicas of buildings. There likely already exists a small-scale model of the building. Like making a molehill out of someone else's mountain, constructing a cake after a building would reduce my edible rendition to the copy of a model. The life of a building is revealed through the effect of its size and the quality of our experience as we move through it. A person who feels that the work is done once an architectural model is made is a sculptor, not an architect.

So instead of making a detail-for-detail rendition of a celebrated building (or any work of art, or science), I ask myself which elements speak to me personally. What in particular do I find interesting or beautiful about it? Is it the overall shape of the structure? Is there a symmetry that makes the structure seem like a glorious, natural eruption? Or is it a provocative asymmetry that makes it stand out in its environment? Is it the odd choice of building materials? Is it the color? The way the light hits it? Or does the encounter strike some distant chord that makes me think of something entirely different? How can I capture the moment of my engagement and put it into my own language? By paying attention to that moment, writing down a few words and a quick sketch, I kick off the beginning of a sugar sculpture or a cake. For instance, from my cakewalk through Barcelona, the undulating modernist curves, the mosaic of pattern of Antoni Gaudi's Casa Batlló, the keystones from the Barcelona Cathedral, and the orange and yellow stripes of the Catalan flag are all discernible in the Barcelona Cake. Just look and you will find them. Ever since that cakewalk I sometimes envision my cakes as massive structures, and in the spirit of the Land of the Brobdingnagians, I shrink down in size, and imagine what it would be like to walk around and live inside them.

I feel this way about the big things as well as the little things, like flowers, for instance. I don't like to replicate them, because I can't improve on nature. Flowers are amazing and complex, with their wild perfumes and colors. So instead of copying a flower petal for petal, I'll give in to nature. Or invent my own flowers. Here's a quotation from a nineteenth-century confectioner with a naturalist bent. He would have hated me.

17

This realist approach to confectionery has inspired some beautiful work, but you shouldn't let these truisms crush your creative impulses. I don't.

I'm attracted by traditionally beautiful decoration, and by the way certain designs work so serenely within their contexts. This enthusiasm is evident in my cakes. But I also love the perceptual shift—the resounding "Aha" of ordinary things, objects from everyday life—suddenly revealing themselves to me. For instance, on a recent trip to my hometown, I was struck by the strange beauty of the playground of my elementary school. Together, the slide, the seesaw, the swings, and the jungle gym had been transformed into a prehistoric sculpture garden. The mundane also caught my eye late one night while working on a cake, when the Argo corn goddess leaped from her yellow box as if to say, "Add a touch of black to that pink and you'll get the magenta you're looking for." Thus began my tradition of late-night chats with the corn goddess. From time to time, the ordinary demands attention by slipping away from its standard framework. Insisting that we not take it for granted, it declares its independence. Have you ever noticed the gargoyles on the building across the street from your house leering at you? The intricate relief work on a brass doorknob? The feminine curves of a bottle of dishwashing liquid? But even more amazing is how something that I have hated for as long as I can remember can suddenly become the apple of my eye.

The Future of Taste

Everything about the house was fine except for the floors, which were covered in linoleum: faux cork, faux parquet, faux brick, faux tile, faux marble. I was appalled. I left dejected, with visions of ripping it all out in one afternoon.

A month later, I returned to the house. After just one look, I had fallen in love with those crazy floors. Something had changed in me. What I had once found repulsive had since become an object of my affection.

I can describe what happened like this. A burning hatred for linoleum burned a linoleum-size hole in my visual sense. It left a cavity, a void in the precise shape of the linoleum, and the void demanded to be filled. The only thing that could fill it was—linoleum. Here's another way of explaining it: after my first encounter with the linoleum, my mind's eye began making reservations for what I was not ready to like right now, but would be in the near future. My instincts are usually good, but this change of heart causes me to challenge my knee-jerk reactions to all kinds of things. By the time I saw the linoleum the second time around, I had changed, and the ugly had become beautiful. I haven't quite gotten there with the interior design of the Metropolitan Opera house, but I will. I like it better every time I see it, and there's still time.

HOW TO USE THIS BOOK

If you're a pro, you might want to go straight to "The Cakes" (page 94). If you have never decorated a cake in your life, you should read everything in this book. Here's a description of what it contains, oriented toward the novice. Use it to decide which parts are for you.

First, read the fabulous introduction, then leaf through the pages and look at all the pictures. Then, I suggest you check the "Tools and Ingredients" section (page 214), which lists every tool needed to make the cakes and all the ingredients, apart from the obvious ones. Most of you will have some of them, some of you will have most of them, but those of you who don't will need to get them. It's an economical and reasonably gadget-free list built on basic kitchen ingredients and cake-decorating materials. Many of these are probably available at your local supermarket, hardware store, kitchenware supplier, or art supply store. If you can't find something, check "Sources and Merchants" (page 218) for ways to get these items by phone or mail order.

If you already know these things or are in a hurry, jump straight to the "Trying Your Hand" section (page 23). This section pertains to the novice and the expert. It consists of a few warm-up exercises to loosen you up, along with my theory on how to develop a good decorating hand. Then move on to "Motifs and Techniques" (page 29). You can think of this section as a visual glossary that will familiarize you with the decorative motifs used in my cakes. It can also serve as an extension to the "Practice" section—you can work up the motifs on parchment paper, baking pans, or your work surface before using them on a cake. Next, "Cake Preparation and Assembly" (page 88) will give you specific instructions on slicing, filling, icing, covering, and constructing the cakes. And with your cake prepped and ready, you will be ready for the best section—"The Cakes" (page 94). If you have already acquainted yourself with the motifs and techniques, you will be way ahead of the game when you start on one of these confectionery endeavors. Finally, the "The Recipes" section (page 199) contains every recipe used for making the cakes, as well as a few of my lifelong favorites. NOTE: *Some of the following recipes request the use of a standing mixer. This is a preference and not a necessity.*

It requires a knowledge of drawing, good taste, and practice to produce neat, elegant designs of ornamentation, but you must not be deterred from trying your hand on account of these difficulties, for you must remember, that industry and perseverance overcome all obstacles.

—C.E. Francatelli,
The Royal Confectioner (1862)

Trying Your Hand

In this chapter you will learn the techniques for making my favorite cake-decorating motifs. Along with the classics, I have added a few of my own invention. Each motif asserts an underlying principle, a personality; each has its reason for being. Later in the book you'll get to know them better as you see how they're used on different cakes. Here I'll tell you why I like to work with them, what they mean to me, how I came up with them, maybe a little bit of history. You should start to think of them as visual ingredients, like flour, eggs, butter, and sugar.

But before discussing the motifs and how to make them, let me suggest a few exercises to loosen you up and get you into a relaxed frame of mind. The first two involve playing with paper, the next two involve thinking, and the third involves drawing.

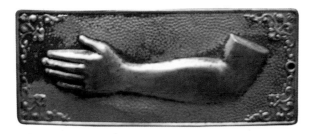

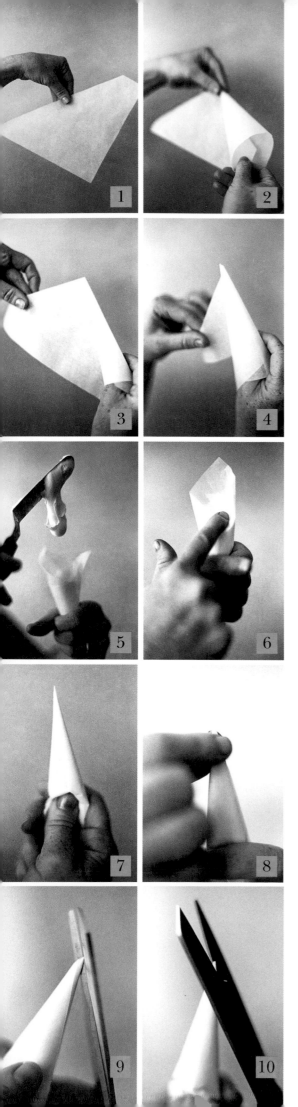

How to Make a Paper Cornetta

1. Hold a triangle of parchment paper in front of you with the point facing downward (see photograph 1).
2. Grasp the outer edges of the right side between the thumb and forefinger of your right hand, and begin to roll in the corner until a partial cornetta is formed (photograph 2).
3. Grasp the outer edges of the left side with your left hand and circle it over your right hand. Move your hands back and forth to adjust the point of the cornetta until it is needle sharp (photographs 3 and 4).
4. Place it in your left hand and drop a small amount of royal icing into the cornetta. Fold down the open ends to seal the cornetta closed (photographs 5 and 6).
5. Hold the sealed cornetta with the point facing upwards (photograph 7).
6. Place scissors precisely horizontal to the vertical cornetta. Cut the tip of the cornetta. You should now have a round decorating tip.

How to Make a Leaf Tip Cornetta

1. Follow steps 1 through 6 above.
2. Flatten the tip between your thumb and forefinger (photograph 8). Cut both sides of the tip to form a point or upside-down "V" (photographs 9 and 10).

THE RHYTHM MANTRA

A sense of rhythm is vital to forming consistent patterns, whether you're making a simple string of pearls or piping an intricate pattern onto your cake. Rhythm can also compensate for underdeveloped fine motor skills. If you think of cake decorating in terms of creating shapes in time, not just in space, you'll be on the right track. You might find it helpful to recite something rhythmic while you work— a mantra of your own choosing. Of course, playing music can help, too.

The Flying Lesson

I piped a stork in royal icing on top of a cake for a baby shower. Hanging from its beak was a small basket, also piped in royal icing. I will never forget that stork, because the cake decorator I was working with looked at it and said, "It's a good stork, but it's not in flight." If you have movement in mind while you do your decorating, it can bring fluidity to your hand. Here's a rhyme to remind you of that.

> *While piping design,*
> *Keep movement in mind.*
> *With this helpful rhyme*
> *comes a fine-looking line.*

Running Dog

This motif is traditionally referred to as a "Running Dog" border. It's a good name because it conjures up rhythm and momentum, which are essential to the art of good cake decorating. Imagine: the race track . . . callused paws slapping gravel—*badadum, badadum, badadum, badadum*—muffled by the cheering masses.

Place a clean sheet of parchment over the drawing on the opposite page and trace it a few times with a pencil. This will help you to understand the significance of rhythm in conjunction with intricate piping.

MOTIFS AND TECHNIQUES

My introduction to cake decorating was rooted in the Italian language because my teachers were from Italy. To this day I often think in Italian while working. A voice in my head guides me with the following words: "Fallo di Nuovo, Margherita, ma uno alla volta, e BENE" ("Do it again, Margaret, but one at a time, and WELL").

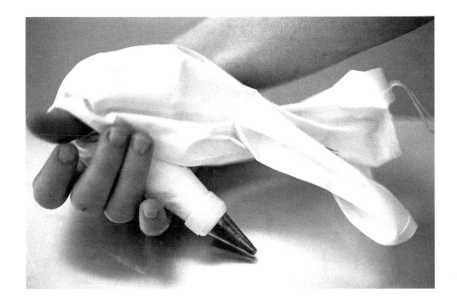

A FEW TIPS:
1. When the instructions tell you to fill your pastry bag, you should fill it only one-third full with icing. This will give you more control of your piping hand.
2. Make sure the icing is pushed down toward the piping end of the bag, and give it a few squeezes to get rid of the air pockets.
3. Practice these techniques as often as possible. You can practice on the side of a baking pan, on the back of a sheet pan, on a sheet of parchment or wax paper, or right on the kitchen table (that's how I do it).

Royal Icing Pearls

You will recognize the pearl border motif in one form or another on many of my cakes, either performing its most common role—which is to create a clean graphic border along the bottom edge of the cake tiers—or as a decorative accompaniment to a larger motif. For example, notice the piping around the flowers of "Decal Recall," or the bubble pattern on "Stripes Are Nice."

I suggest that whenever you have some extra royal icing and a little time on your hands, you practice the pearl border motif. It's a great way to hook into the rhythm mantra. And since it's used on many of the cakes, practicing it is like the dress rehearsal before the performance.

Pearls are associated with St. Margaret of Antioch, and with Cleopatra, who dropped a large pearl into her wine glass. In art, a necklace of pearls is also a common adornment of the Earthly Venus. Who was she? Fifteenth-century Florentine humanists embraced the idea of the twin Venuses, expressing two kinds of love— Earthly and Heavenly. (This concept was originally formulated in Plato's discussion of the nature of love in the Symposium.*) And Pearl was the name of Hester Prynne's illegitimate daughter.*

DIRECTIONS:
1. Fill a pastry bag with royal icing and attach a #7 round decorating tip.
2. Hold the bottom third of the pastry bag at a 45-degree angle just above a work surface. Apply pressure and watch a pearl emerge from the tip. When the pearl is rotund and lovely, pull the tip away with a slight clipping motion. Begin a second pearl where the first one ended. Be careful not to damage the integrity of the first one. Practice this a few times.
3. Now you are ready. Pipe out an even string of pearls along the base of a cake. The rhythm is in basic 4/4 time: 1,2,3,4, 1,2,3,4, 1,2,3,4, 1,2,3,4.

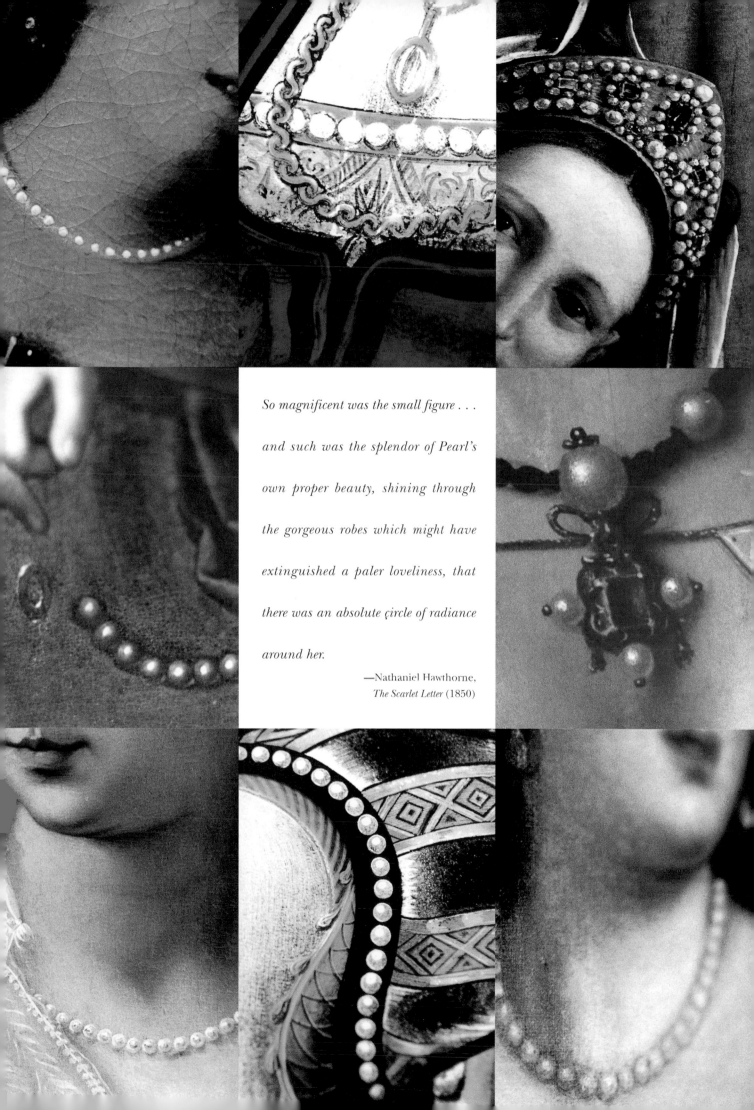

So magnificent was the small figure . . .

and such was the splendor of Pearl's

own proper beauty, shining through

the gorgeous robes which might have

extinguished a paler loveliness, that

there was an absolute çircle of radiance

around her.

—Nathaniel Hawthorne,
The Scarlet Letter (1850)

Scallop Shells

The scallop shell is so familiar that you don't have to be a confectioner to recognize it as an unofficial symbol for cake decorating. It should be certified. For this reason, I love it. However, I am careful when using it on my cakes. Its scalloped edge can be distracting. When used unwisely, it can turn into the epitome of heavy-handed design at its worst. Instead, I use it with more minimal designs. It requires the same technique as the pearl border.

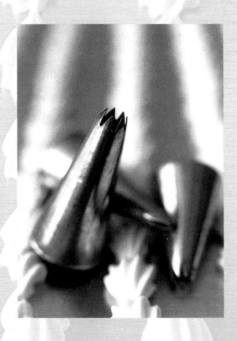

DIRECTIONS:
1. Attach a #18 shell tip to a filled pastry bag.
2. Hold the pastry bag at a 45-degree angle against the cake base.
3. Begin piping an even string of shells, slightly lifting the tip from the surface to form a rise, like the arched back of a snail. As with the pearl border, think 4/4 time.

Scallop shells are associated with Venus, born of the sea, who floated ashore holding one in her hand. Dolphins and hippocampi (fabulous sea creatures that were part horse, part fish) draw the scallop-shell carriage of Neptune and Galatea. The scallop shell is the badge worn by pilgrims to the shrine of Santiago de Compostela in Spain and is also associated with St. Roch. During the golden age of legend, when humanity's simple needs were supplied by nature, shells were used as cups and platters.

Swags

Here is the architectural swag I talked about in the introduction. Swags have a sort of jocular rhythm, but they also have a sobering effect on me—a reminder that cakes are constructed much like miniature buildings. Swags convey the structural reality of a cake, and ground the overall design with style and grace. *Svagga* means to "sway" or "swagger" in Norwegian.

DIRECTIONS:

1. Place a clean sheet of parchment over the opposite page, and trace these swags with a pencil. Remove the tracing from the page and adhere it to your work surface by piping bits of royal icing in each of the four corners of your parchment paper.
2. Attach a #7 round tip to the filled pastry bag. With pastry bag in hand, pretend to pipe over the tracing of swags, to get the feeling for it. Picture how real fabric swags fall delicately from curtains on a stage. Think of how gravity would gently draw down the center of swag. Remember your rhythm: 1,2,3,4, 1,2,3,4.
3. Pipe a necklace of pearls from left to right over your tracing. The small pearls at the top left and top right require less pressure to the pastry bag. The larger pearls toward the middle require more pressure.
4. To achieve the coiled effect of the swag, repeat step 3, except this time add a clockwise coiling motion to the pearling technique. Practice over and over and over. (Rhythm mantra!)
5. Now try it on a cake.

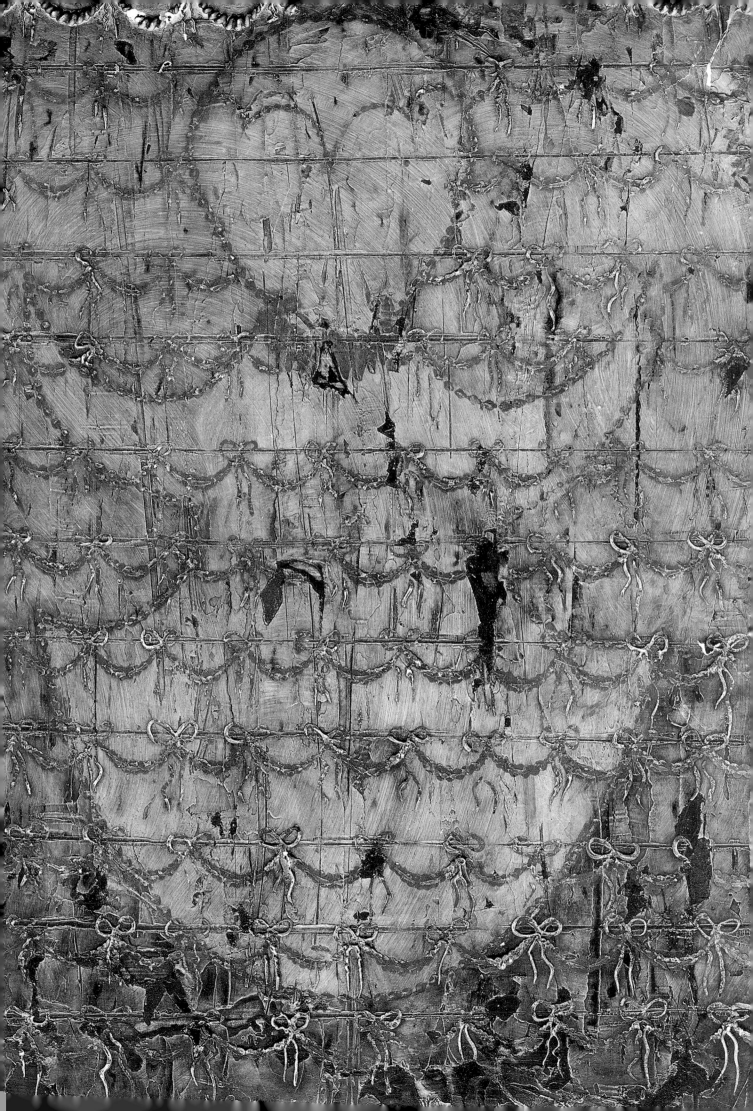

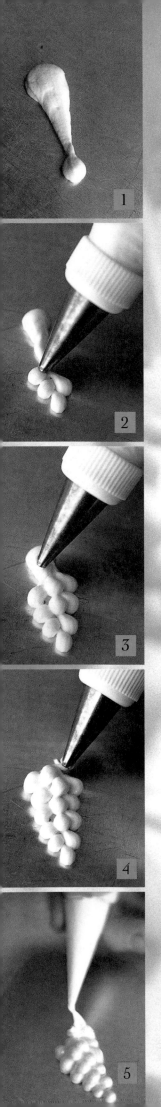

Royal Icing Grapes

Like swags, grapes are often used as architectural decorations. I like to think of fake fruit in architecture as man's way of honoring the natural environment in which he has just erected a huge nonorganic structure. But on my cakes, royal icing grapes are an homage to the decorative arts and architecture. From real juicy grapes on the vine to marble grape bas-relief, to glass grapes on a chandelier or metalwork grapes on a wall sconce, it's just one more step to royal icing grapes on a cake.

These can be piped directly onto the cake, or they can be made in advance and stored in an airtight container. Here is the method for making them in advance.

DIRECTIONS:

1. Cut a sheet of parchment paper the size of the bottom side of a standard baking sheet.
2. Attach a #7 round tip to a pastry bag filled with royal icing.
3. Pipe an upside-down teardrop or the top part of an exclamation point. At the pointed end of the teardrop, pipe a pearl (like the exclamation point) (see photograph 1).
4. Pipe two pearls above the first one, then three pearls above them, then four, like an upside-down "pyramid" of grapes, and maybe a few more on top of that (photographs 2 to 4).
5. For the leaves, prepare a leaf-tip cornetta and pipe royal icing leaves onto the grapes (photograph 5).
6. Let the grapes dry overnight. When they are dry, lift them from the parchment paper and store them in an airtight container.
7. Apply the dried grapes to your cake with a little dab of royal icing.

38

In secular art, **grapes** are often associated with Bacchus, the god of wine, who wears a crown of vine leaves and grapes, and with Vincent of Saragossa, the patron saint of wine growers. In Christian art, grapes are the symbol of Eucharistic wine. St. Augustine likened Christ to a cluster of grapes from the Promised Land that had been put under a wine press. Grapes were also used as a purely decorative motif and are found on early Roman sarcophagi, in the wall paintings of Roman catacombs, in Byzantine mosaics, and in medieval stained-glass work.

Polka Dots

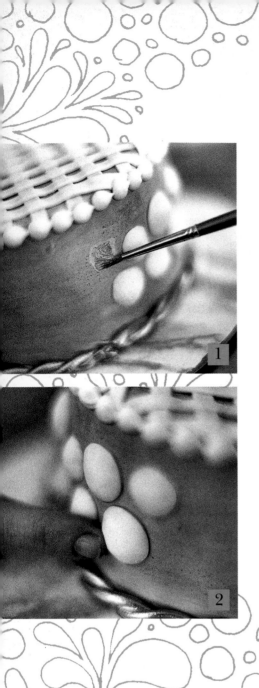

Polka dots are often associated with the polka, the nineteenth-century Bohemian dance, as dancers often wore clothing with dotted patterning. When in doubt, use polka dots—they're a smart way to fill an empty space, and they're easy to make. But for this motif to work well, you must be thoughtful in your placement of the dots—they can look rushed and clumsy. I make polka dots by rolling lots of sugar-paste balls in different sizes and flattening them out by hand. But this is a time-consuming method; there are other ways to make polka dots. You can cut them out with purpose-made cutters, use the open end of decorating tubes, or find other suitable round objects. Look around your kitchen.

DIRECTIONS:

1. Dust a smooth, clean work surface with cornstarch.
2. Roll out a thin sheet of sugar paste with a small rolling pin.
3. Cut out polka dots in various sizes—nickels, dimes, Altoids, and Advils. (See above suggestions for cutters.)
4. Mark the placement of dots on your cake with a small paintbrush dipped in water. This will make the sugar paste or marzipan sticky, so the dots will adhere to the surface (see photograph 1).
5. Apply the polka dots to your cake (photograph 2).

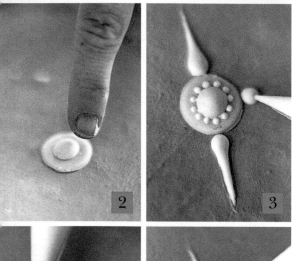

Atomic Starbursts

This motif was originally inspired by the magnificent keystones in the rib vaulting of La Seu (the Barcelona cathedral). Keystones are downright mighty. As the topmost block of an arch, the keystone locks the other stones into place and ensures that the entire monument does not come crashing down. They can support tremendous symbolic weight. But they also reminded me of other things. My modernist sensibilities shredded through centuries of the grounding principles of architecture, landing me first in the retro-space realm of George Jetson and ultimately in the kitchen, where atomic-age imagery had entered the commercial sphere, from patterns on drinking glasses to the starburst clock on the wall of American homes in the early 1960s.

DIRECTIONS:

1. On a clean surface dusted with cornstarch, roll out a sheet of pastillage with a small rolling pin.
2. Cut out a circle using a small round cutter of your choice (see photograph 1).
3. Mark the placement of starbursts on your cake with a damp paintbrush, then adhere the cut-out dots to the cake.
4. Pipe a large pearl into the center of the starburst (photograph 2).
5. Fill a paper cornetta with a small amount of royal icing. Cut the end of the cornetta straight across to create a small round tip, approximately the size of a #3 round decorating tip.
6. Pipe icing teardrops around the circumference of each dot at these positions: 12:00, 1:30, 3:00, 4:30, 6:00, 7:30, 9:00, and 10:30 (photographs 3 and 4).
7. Pipe small pearls in between the teardrops.
8. When the icing is dry, gild the teardrops with gold dust and the pearls with pearl dust (photograph 6).

42

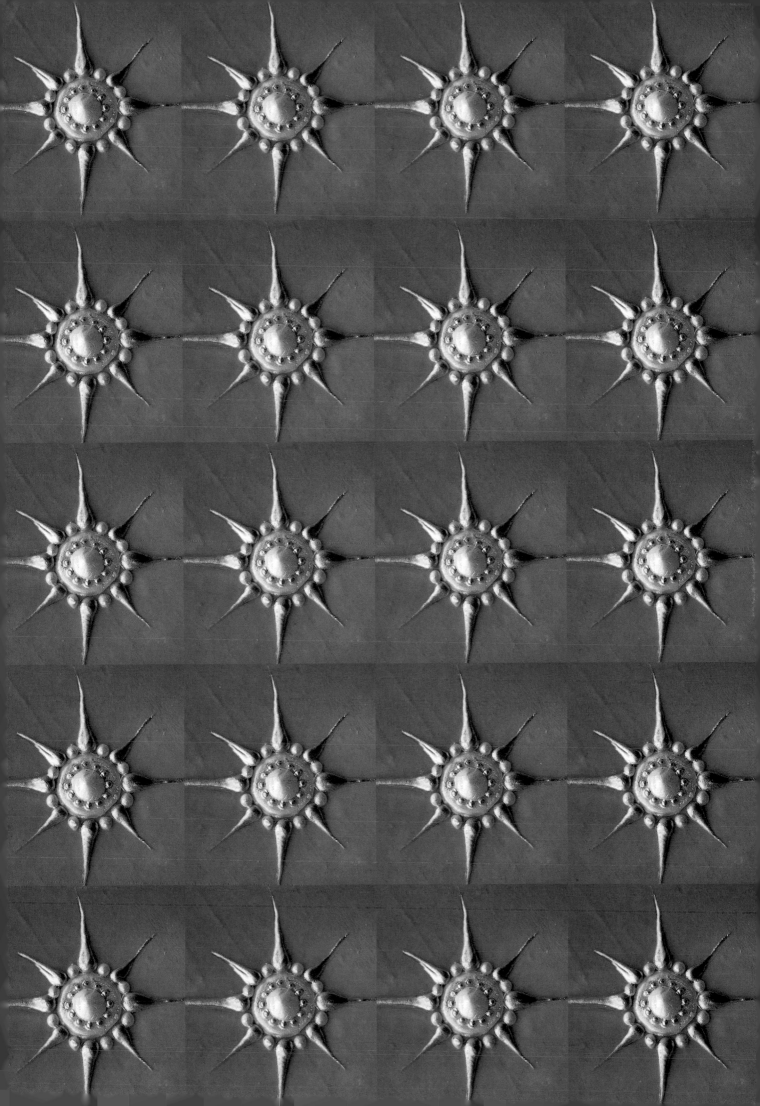

Star is stella *in Italian, which you can see in the word "constellation" (meaning "an arrangement with stars"). From the ancient religions of Persia and Babylonia to the Greeks and Romans, stars were thought of as divinities. The planetary gods (Venus, Mercury, and so forth) were sometimes pictured with a star on their brow. Bacchus flung the crown of Ariadne into the heavens, where it became a constellation of stars. Early Renaissance art often depicted a star on the shoulder of the Virgin's cloak, and it's said that Thomas Aquinas wore a star on his habit.*

Rococo Relief

Rococo is derived from the word "rock" (*rocca* in Italian; *roche* in French) and refers to an eighteenth-century style of elaborate, fanciful ornamentation that imitates foliage and scroll work, as well as the scallop shell, an attribute of the Christian Saint Roch (1293–1327).

Rococo sometimes gets a bum rap. Often misunderstood, it can be perceived as outright gaudy—the Liberace of decorative styles. My own earlier attempts at beautifying cakes with lavish sugar-work shells and swirls landed me in a heavy-handed mess. On the other hand, the examples on the following pages, while a bit over the top, are beautifully busy, rather stately and elegant.

The moldings on my "Baroque in Patent Leather" cake (page 164) were shaped by hand in pastillage, which is very difficult to do. Here is an easier way that still looks great.

FOR PRACTICE:

1. This technique is easier with a softer mix of royal icing. To prepare it, add about one teaspoon of water to each cup of icing and blend well in a mixing bowl.
2. Fill your pastry bag and attach a #7 round tip.
3. Place a sheet of parchment over page 47 or 49 and trace the rococo pattern in royal icing with loose, sweeping motions.

DIRECTIONS:

1. Look at your undecorated surface first and picture where you want to pipe the relief. It may help you to sketch the pattern onto the cake surface with a paintbrush dipped in a little water.
2. Now, pipe the design onto the cake with . . . rhythm.

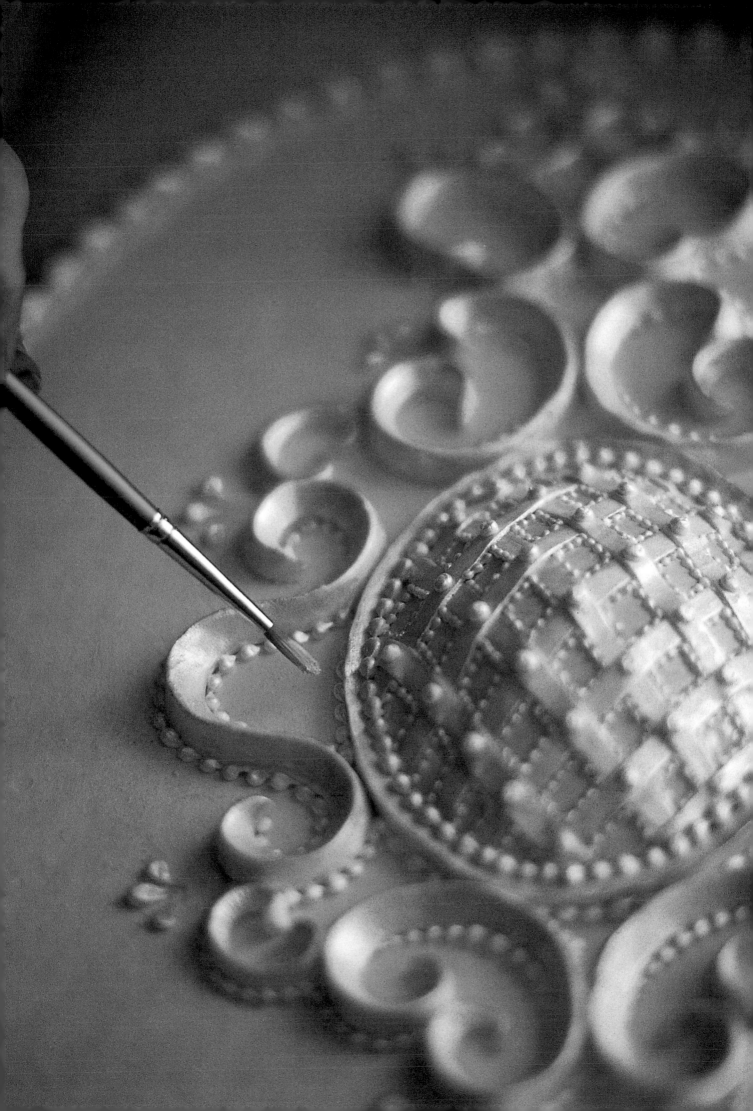

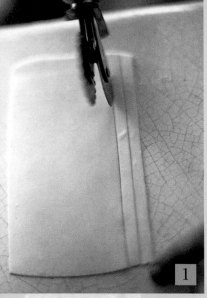

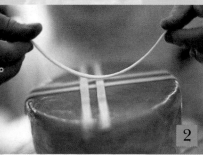

Crosshatching

I was crouching beneath the low ceiling of a crypt in a twelfth-century Belgian church. It was an eerie combination of light and dark. The whitewashed walls seemed out of place in this subterranean vault, until I realized they had once been covered in fresco. A series of arches were supported by short stocky pillars bearing the remains of a delicate cross-hatched relief pattern. Light caught my eye from a dim flank of the crypt. It was reflecting off a gold vessel in a showcase, which was placed against an even stockier pillar. The vessel carried the same crosshatching as the pillars, but it was studded with emeralds. It was a reliquary containing the bones of a saint. The crosshatched pattern became etched in my mind, and soon I saw it on sidewalks, in metal shop gates, in gardens with grapes growing on them, even in the chain-link fence surrounding the construction site across the street from my hotel.

The term crosshatching, also referred to as latticework, is derived from the Greek word for the Milky Way, *Galaxias* (also meaning "galaxy"; likewise, *gala* means "milk," and *laxias*, "lactic"). Like a constellation crossing the sky, a lattice is comprised of crossing strips, and like the "milky" constellation, the word lattice is associated with *latte*, the Italian word for "milk." In Italian, *latticino* refers to foods prepared with milk and to interlacing threadlike patterns of white glass used in glass making.

Like polka dots, crosshatching is another great way to fill a space that needs decoration. Like the swag motif, it has structural undertones, and like curlicues it can be seen everywhere (once you look). Crosshatching can add a nice complexity to the cake surface.

DIRECTIONS:

1. Dust a clean work surface with cornstarch. Roll out a thin 1-inch square sheet of sugar paste.
2. With a damp paintbrush, sketch a crosshatched pattern one line at a time.
3. With a pastry cutter or paring knife, cut a ¼-inch-wide strip of sugar paste (see photograph 1). Cover the remaining sheet of sugar paste with plastic wrap while you perform the next step.
4. Gently lift the sugar-paste strip from your work surface and apply it over your sketched pattern (photograph 2).
5. Repeat steps 2 through 4 until the decorating is complete (photographs 3 and 4).

NOTE: *Work quickly, since sugar paste will dry out.*

In Egyptian mythology, **rope** is often associated with the afterlife or with bondage. In Christian art and culture, it can figure as a symbol of betrayal (Christ was bound and led by rope on the road to Calvary), remorse (Judas, overcome with guilt, hanged himself from rope), despair (one of the vices), or penitence.

Sugar-Paste Roping

This is a great alternative to the more conventional methods for bordering the bottom edge of the cake tiers. This is not utilitarian rope that decorates my cakes, the kind of fibrous rope that might be seen flung over the bow of a whaling ship, or the rope that holds up your hammock. This is decorative rope, and sugar paste lends itself beautifully to a satin-finish decorative rope. I see sugar-paste roping as a confectionery rendering of the satin rope that dangles from the wrist of a royal subject or loops from the high waistline of a medieval dress—or of the velvet rope that supports the petal-soft tassels used in Louis XIV window treatments.

DIRECTIONS:

1. On a clean surface dusted with cornstarch, knead a handful of sugar paste until it's nice and pliable.
2. Roll out a long strand of sugar paste about the width of a pencil (or as thin as you can get it without breaking it). Work quickly to keep the sugar paste from cracking. This takes a little practice (see photograph 1).
3. Cut the strand evenly in half and place the strands parallel to each other.
4. Pinch the two together at the left end.
5. With your left hand, begin rolling the pinched left end of the sugar paste toward you while holding the right end in place. The sugar paste will automatically coil into a rope (photograph 2).
6. Dampen the base of your cake with a paintbrush.
7. Gently lift the sugar-paste rope and place it along the border of the cake (photograph 3).

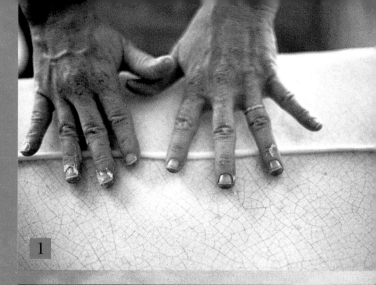

1

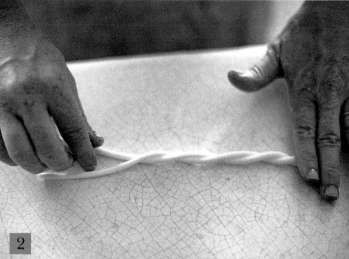

2

3

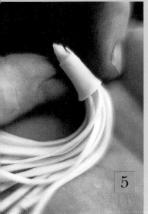

Sugar-Paste Tassels

Velvet is beautiful, but Vermeer's rendering of it is a representation of velvet that's better than the real thing. That's why I am more interested in artistic renditions. Such a portrayal brings the feeling of eye-popping incredulity—a rapturous longing to understand what seems impossible to achieve. How could a person paint something so magnificent?

In Italian, *coi fiocchi* means "with tassels," signifying something of excellence. And tassels are beautiful. They are sumptuous. They implore you to touch them and run your fingers through them. My sugar-paste tassels are made in honor of those painters whose renderings of tassels inspired in me the longing to touch.

DIRECTIONS:

1. Roll out a very thin sheet of sugar paste.
2. Square off the edges with a paring knife.
3. Cut a comblike sequence of 1-inch-long parallel lines as close together as you possibly can without breaking them off (see photograph 1).
4. Gently roll up the comb into a tassel (photograph 2).
5. Squeeze the top end together (photograph 3).
6. Lift it, give it a little shake, and let gravity do its thing (photograph 3).
7. Cut a small strip from the remaining sugar paste and wrap it around the top end of the tassel (photographs 4 and 5).
8. Attach your tassel to the end of a sugar-paste rope.

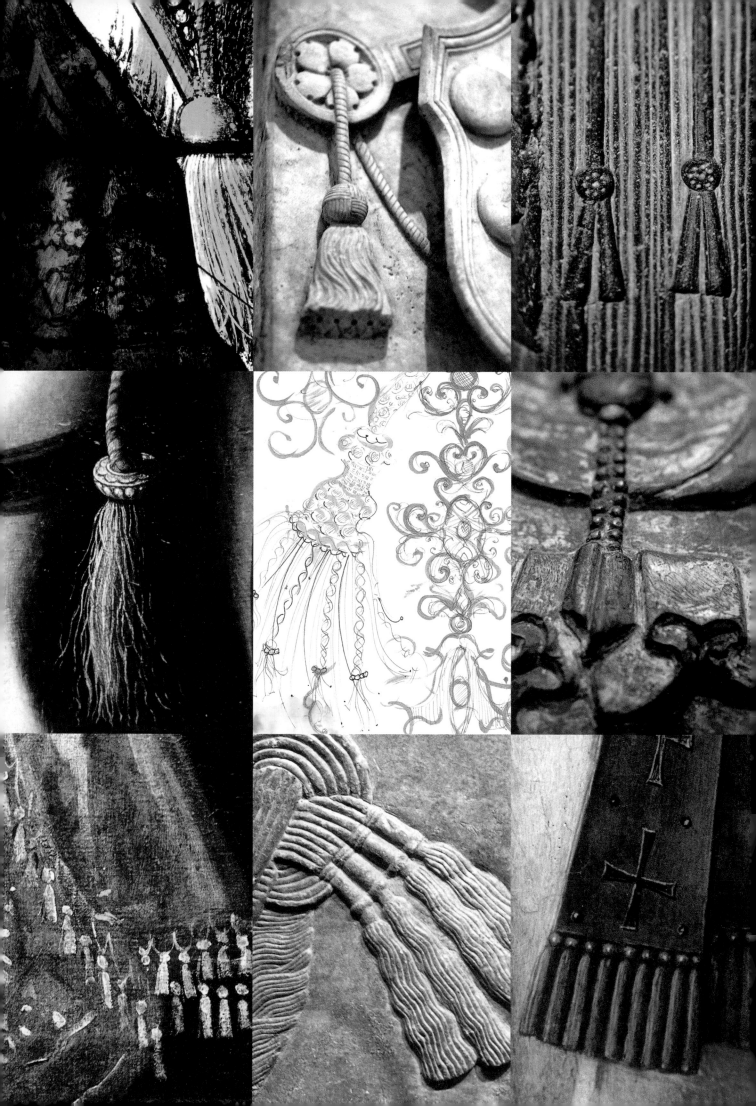

Curlicues

The world is teeming with curlicues (from the Italian *riccio*, for "curl," "lock, "or the "hedgehog" that curls beneath its pelt). I guarantee that if you start looking around for them, you will agree. Aside from the countless examples of curlicues in the arts, the curlicue is one of the finest examples of form following function. It functions beautifully in the industrial and domestic realms, as well as in the purely aesthetic. Commonly wrought in iron, curlicues snake through our fire escapes and the bars of our windows. They twirl through fences, separating us from our neighbors, and swirl beneath the handrail leading to the door of a house to protect us from slipping off into the rose bushes. Curlicues buttress our street lamps, mailboxes, and awnings; they pretty up our lawn furniture, hotplates, coffee-mug holders, and jewelry. Pastillage curlicues, though good-looking suggestions of structure, offer only the illusion of support.

DIRECTIONS:

1. Roll out a thin, 2-inch by 5-inch rectangle of pastillage. It should be about the thickness of a CD-case cover or a hard-shell floppy disk.
2. With a paring knife, cut an even $1/2$-inch-wide strip across the long side of the pastillage. Cover the remainder with plastic wrap to prevent it from drying out.
3. Quickly prop the pastillage strip on its side. Wrap one end around the handle end of a paintbrush and begin curling (see photograph 1). Repeat the process on the opposite side (photograph 2).
4. Once you have achieved an elegant curl, remove the brush and leave the curl to dry overnight (photographs 3 to 5).
5. When all the curlicues are dry, apply them to your cake with royal icing.

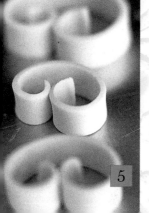

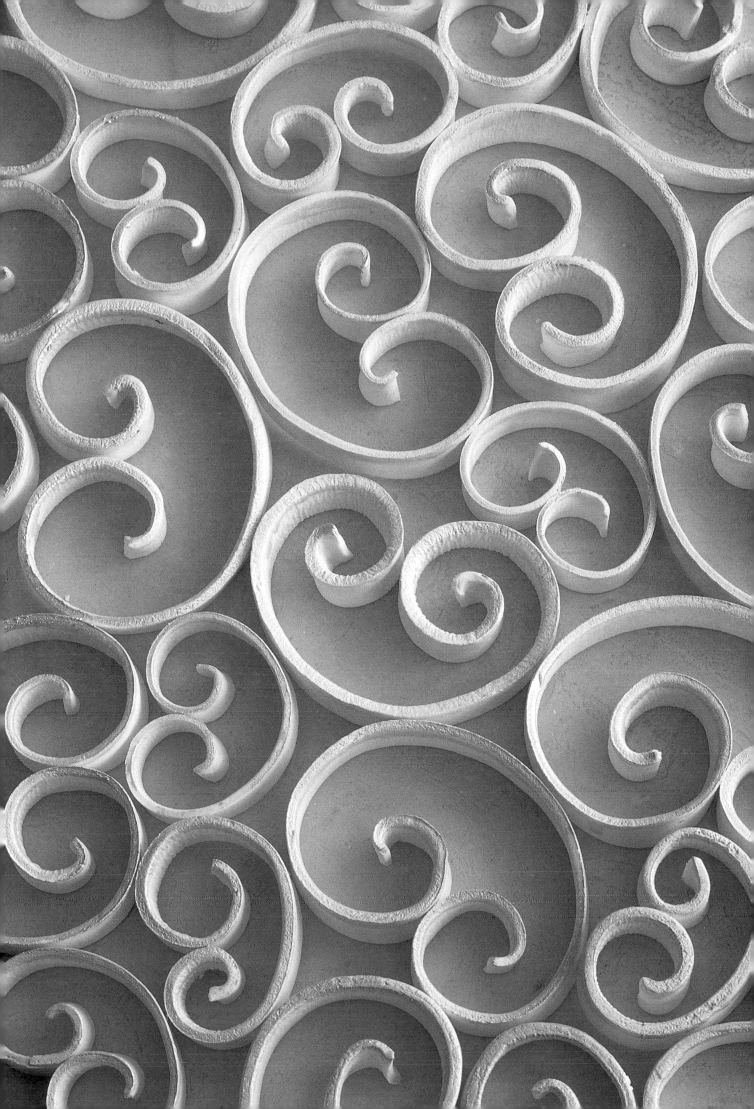

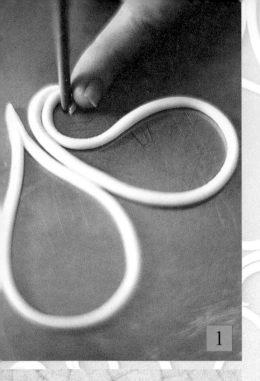

1

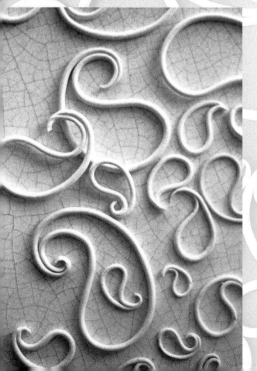

Pastillage Paisleys

The paisley is a swirling abstract pattern—a sinuous network of curves that snakes within the contours of a stylized palmette leaf. Used over the centuries in Persian rugs, intricate classical moldings, vases, fresco paintings, and the hand-woven shawls made in the Scottish city of Paisley, by the 1970s the paisley had made its way to the contact paper that lined my parents' silverware drawer. The Pastillage Paisleys flanking the ledges of "Akbar's Cake" (page 140) are my Eastern-design counterpart to the curlicue buttressing on some of my other cakes.

DIRECTIONS:

1. On a smooth surface dusted with cornstarch, roll out a 6-inch-long spaghetti-thin string of pastillage. (Make it as thin as you can without breaking it.)
2. Loop one end back to the other and pinch the two ends together to create a big teardrop (see photograph 1).
3. With a gum-paste tool or the handle end of a paint-brush, gently wrap the point of the teardrop around the brush and twist until it starts to form a spiral, thus creating a paisley shape (photograph 1).
4. Make as many more as you need. Let them dry in place overnight.

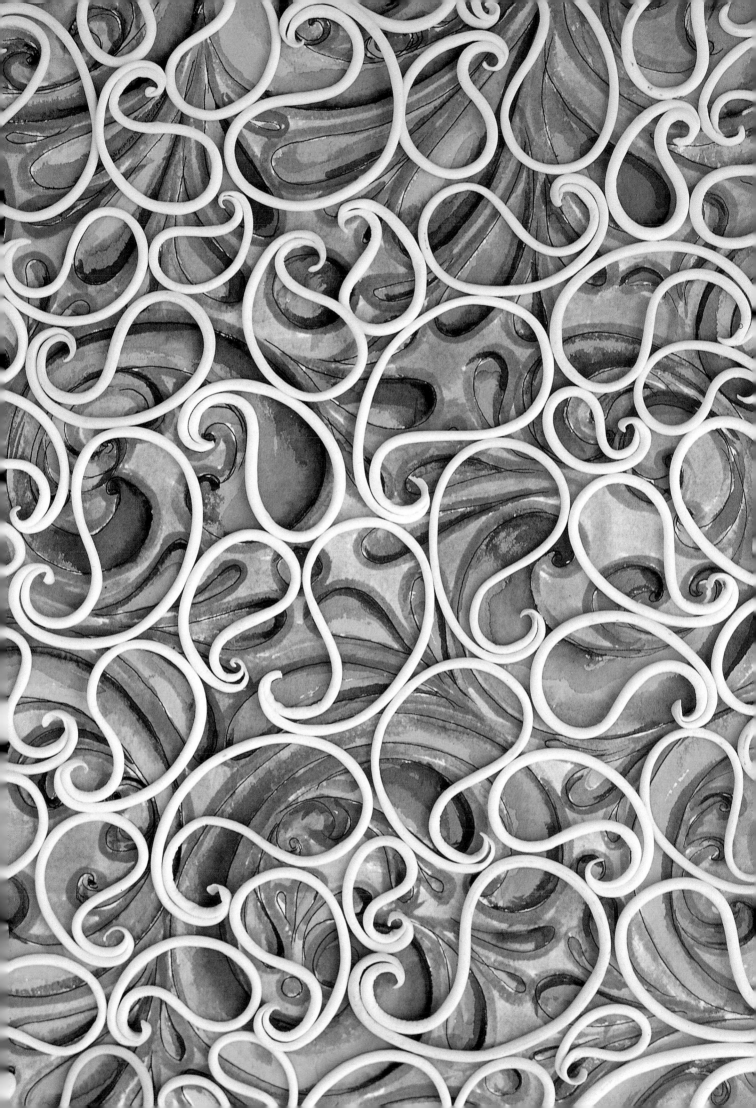

Pastillage Ursulines

Nathaniel Hawthorne's *Scarlet Letter* tells the story of **Hester Prynne**, who, because she bore a child out of wedlock, is ostracized by her village and regarded as the personification of sin. The legend of **St. Ursula** tells the story of Ursula, a German princess who led a pilgrimage of 11,000 virgins to Rome. (It was a long journey, which included stopping off to pick up the queen of Sicily.) On their way home, they were overtaken by the Huns, and all 11,000 virgins were slaughtered. When Ursula refused to be the bride of the leader of the Huns, he pierced her heart with a golden arrow.

With the legend of St. Ursula, one symbolic image of piety embodies the 11,000 lives. With Hester Prynne, one life serves as the embodiment of impiety, and as a warning to countless others.

When the Ursuline virgins lost their individuality, they became the symbol of virtue to be emulated by the young and the pure. For the fallen Hester Prynne:

Giving up her individuality, she would become the general symbol of woman's frailty and sinful passion . . . thus the young and the pure would be taught to look at her, with the scarlet letter flaming on her breast . . . as the figure, the body, the reality of sin. And over her grave, the infamy that she must carry thither must be her only monument.

Though Ursula is venerated and Hester damned, their images in art and literature divulge a similar enigmatic poise. I relate a distant gaze, and pious anonymity, and the self-contained majesty of the Ursuline reliquaries in museums and churches, to Hawthorne's description of the stupefying entrance of Hester Prynne:

Hester Prynne's term of confinement was now at an end. Her prison door was thrown open, and she came forth into the sunshine, which falling on all alike, seemed . . . as if meant for no other purpose than to reveal the scarlet letter on her breast . . . Her attire, which indeed, she had wrought for the occasion, in

prison, and had modeled much after her own fancy, seemed to express the attitude of her spirit, the desperate recklessness of her mood, by its wild and picturesque peculiarity . . . It was so artistically done . . . but greatly beyond what was allowed by the sumptuary regulations of the colony. But now with this unattended walk from her prison door, began the daily custom: and she must either sustain and carry it forward by the ordinary resources of her nature, or sink beneath it . . . It may be true, that, to a sensitive observer, there was something exquisitely painful in it . . . Those who had before known her, and had expected to behold her dimmed, and obscured by a disastrous cloud, were astonished, and even startled, to perceive how her beauty shone out and made a halo of misfortune and ignominy . . . It had the effect of a spell taking her out of the ordinary relations with humanity, and enclosing her in a sphere by herself . . . characterized by a certain state of dignity, rather than by delicate, evanescent, and indescribable grace . . . never had Hester Prynne appeared more lady-like.

The dresslike sugar draperies of this motif are an offshoot from a series of sculptures I made about the relationship between Hester Prynne and the legend of St. Ursula. Although these motifs resemble fabric clinging to the contours of the human body, I don't try to make them look like the actual fabric. Instead, I make them resemble painterly and sculptural interpretations of fabric and dress, such as the Gothic stone sculpture of the Virgin above the central doorway of Reims cathedral in France, or most often like the enigmatic polychrome wood-carved drapery in medieval sculpture.

DIRECTIONS:

1. On a clean surface dusted with cornstarch, roll out a thin sheet of pastillage.
2. Using a paring knife, cut out a bell shape.
3. Gently fold the pastillage onto itself so it resembles drapes.
4. Lift it from the surface and adhere it to your cake with a little bit of royal icing. Finesse the drapery by hand to make it look more like real fabric.

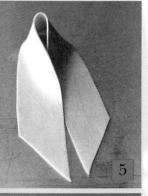

Sugar Bows

Sugar and spice and (the unspecified) everything nice must include sugar bows. Charming, graceful, playful, and sweet, the sugar bow is an emblem of feminine delicacy, and a miniature sugar sculpture—each fold and each crease in a bow reveals a facet of its character. But I see the corseted, tightly wound epicenter of the bow as a symbol of self-containment. When a bow is not made to perfection, it tells the story of a little girl with scraped knees and chocolate ice cream on the sides of her mouth—an image very dear to my heart. But for the "It's All About the Bows" cake to hold its own, the bows must be made to perfection.

DIRECTIONS:

These directions are for the small bow used on the top tier of "It's All About the Bows" (page 122). The measurements for the remaining bows are: bottom tier, $9^1/_2$ inches long by 3 inches high; second tier, $8^1/_2$ inches long by 2 inches high; third tier, $7^1/_2$ inches long by $1^1/_2$ inches high.

1. With scissors, cut two 2-inch-wide strips from a standard-sized sheet of paper towel. Roll them up into a coil and tape them closed. On a smooth surface dusted with cornstarch, roll out a thin sheet of pastillage. With a paring knife, cut a $6^1/_2$-inch by $1^1/_4$-inch pastillage rectangle (see photograph 1).

2. Place a paper towel roll onto the pastillage strip, near one end. Moisten the middle of the strip with a damp paintbrush, making it just a little sticky. Pick up one end of the sugar-paste strip, pinching it between your thumb and index finger, fold it over the paper towel roll, and attach it to the sticky middle (photograph 2).

3. Repeat for the other end of the sugar-paste strip, thus creating a bow.

4. Cut a $^1/_2$-inch by 2-inch strip from the remaining pastillage, place it over the pinched middle of the bow, and wrap it around it. Finesse the folds of the bow and turn the edges upward (photographs 3 and 4).

5. Begin the tail by cutting a $^3/_4$-inch by 6-inch strip from the remaining pastillage. Cut the ends of the strip on a diagonal. Grasp the tail gently in the middle, lift it, and let gravity do its thing. Place it back onto the work surface (photograph 5).

6. Moisten the top of the tail (where the fold is) with a wet paintbrush, and place the bow on top of the tail.

7. Let the bow dry overnight. When it's dry, remove the paper towels (photograph 6).

8. Attach the bow to your cake with royal icing.

Basket Weave

This is another very conventional motif. I have included it because the basket-weave technique is an outright optical illusion, and I find that very intriguing. Like polka dots, the basket-weave pattern can hold its own as the dominant feature of a cake. It is a bold design lending itself to a variety of colors, and it just works for me.

Roman myth has a tale of the infant Erichthonius shut in a basket by Minerva. Her daughters, peeking against orders, were so horrified to find that the infant had serpent's tails for legs that they jumped off the Acropolis; the infant grew up to become king of Athens. Judeo-Christian culture has its infant in a basket too—Moses. The basket was associated with Christ's feeding of the wedding guests, and later with St. Dorothea of Cappadocia, who is depicted with a basket of apples or roses.

DIRECTIONS:

1. Attach a #47 basket-weave tip to a filled pastry bag.
2. With the nonjagged edge of the tip facing toward you, pipe a vertical line from the top to the bottom of the cake tier (photograph 1).
3. Turn the pastry bag around so the jagged edge now faces you and pipe a series of 1-inch horizontal strips across the vertical line from top to bottom. Place the strips approximately ¹/2 inch apart, or the width of the pastry tip (photograph 2).
4. Pipe another vertical line parallel to the first line, about a ¹/2 inch away (photograph 3).
5. Pipe another series of 1-inch horizontal strips to fill in the empty spaces (photograph 4).
6. Continue until you've worked your way around the tier.

Marzipan Fruits

An arrangement of marzipan fruits set on a pedestal is a spectacle to behold. Marzipan or sugar work *trionfi di tavole*—magnificent sculptural table designs—were traditional features of the formal banquets in the baroque palaces of Rome. In Italy, especially in Tuscany and Umbria, ceramic *trionfi* have been made by the local artisans for centuries. They can be as simple as a couple of the lemoniest lemons you have ever seen on a tile, a bowl, a plate, or a cup. But the motifs have expanded beyond fruits to include arabesques, fleurs-de-lis, and dragons painted onto ceremonial plates, goblets, jugs, and chemist's jars or sculpted in bas-relief patterns onto candlesticks, votive plaques, and inkstands. Either way, these ceramics are baked with a shiny glaze that reminds me of sugar syrup. The rendering of the fruits makes them appear frozen in a moment of ideal beauty, blemishes and all. I was on a cakewalk through Cortona when I said to myself, "One day, I am going to make a cake covered with fruits just like these."

DIRECTIONS:

1. Prepare a smooth surface dusted with cornstarch.
2. For LEMONS: Mix a few drops of lemon-yellow food coloring into a handful of marzipan. Knead until incorporated.
   For LIMES: Mix a few drops of leaf green and a few drops of lemon yellow food coloring into a handful of marzipan. Knead until incorporated.
   For ORANGES: Mix a few drops of orange food coloring into a handful of marzipan. Knead until incorporated.
3. Roll out a rope of marzipan the width of a dime. Cut 1/2-inch slices from the rope.
4. Shape into little marbles with both hands.
5. With a marzipan tool (or a Phillips-head screwdriver), poke "stems" into both sides of the fruit. This completes the basic preparation of the oranges.
   For LEMONS and LIMES: Pinch each poked end, creating a lemonlike pointed shape.

Burnishing Fruits

1. Add a few drops of brown food coloring to 1 cup of water in a bowl, until the color is watery brown. Too much brown will make the fruit appear overripe or rotten.
2. Immerse your hands in the bowl, covering them with the burnishing water.
3. Burnish the marzipan fruits by gently rolling them around in your hands.
4. Adhere the fruits to your cake.

Ceramic Glaze

1. Mix 1/4 cup of Grand Marnier (or other liqueur) into 3 tablespoons of piping gel. Using a small whisk or a fork, mix out the lumps until it becomes a clear syrupy glaze.
2. Apply this "ceramic glaze" to the fruits with a paintbrush.

Fruit is associated with Ceres, the goddess of agriculture, of abundance, and of summer. In sixteenth-century engravings, an ape with a piece of fruit in its mouth represents the attribute of taste; in other contexts, a bowl of fruit sometimes stands for the virtue of Charity: angels brought baskets of fruit to Christ in the wilderness. In seventeenth-century Nederlandish paintings a cornucopia of fruit is depicted with images of Vertumnus and Pomona, the protectors of orchards and ripening fruit.

Sugar Mosaic

Byzantine mosaics were built with stone, marble, and colored glass tile. The transcendental quality of the Byzantine mosaic was achieved in part by adhering gold leaf to the underside of the glass tiles before pressing them into wet plaster. Gold leaf has a magical way of emitting light while storing it at the same time, so concealing the gold leaf behind the surface of the glass yields mosaics lit from within.

But since pastillage and sugar paste is opaque, I instead fixed the gold leaf to the front of the tiles, creating an entirely different effect. This method of applying it to the exterior is more akin to the flat gold-leaf backgrounds of painted icons from Byzantium.

My sugar mosaics are built the old-fashioned way—one tile at a time. The *tesserae* (individual tiles) are painted with food coloring, cut to size, and fixed to the cake with sugar and royal icing. It is difficult to do and takes a long time, so here is an easier way.

DIRECTIONS:
1. Cover your cake with a thin sheet of marzipan.
2. With a large paintbrush dipped in simple syrup, lightly moisten the exterior of the marzipan-covered cake.
3. Cover the cake with a layer of sugar paste (of standard thickness).
4. Design a mosaic pattern (see the background of this page) by pressing carefully into the sugar-paste surface with a marzipan tool, the blunt edge of a paring knife or butter knife, or assorted gum-paste cutters. Be careful not to cut all the way through the sugar paste.
5. Fill in these creases with a soft mix of royal icing "mortar." Wipe away excess icing.
6. Paint the tiles as desired with food coloring and gild them with gold dust.

Sugar-Paste Marbles

I love these. As with polka dots, when you're in doubt, you can also use sugar-paste marbles. You can mix any color into them. You can even marbleize the marbles (see "How to Marbleize Sugar Paste or Marzipan," page 91). They look great, they are sweet and chewy to eat, and they're oh-so-easy to make. They can also be made of marzipan.

DIRECTIONS:

1. Roll out a rope of sugar paste the width of a roll of dimes.
2. Cut it into sections, all one size or varied sizes.
3. Shape each section into a ball with both hands.
4. Adhere the marbles to your cake by wetting the target area with a damp paintbrush. Place them on the top tier for a cake topper, or along the ledges of other tiers.

Faux Daisies

I call these faux daisies because they do resemble daisies. But they are actually made with a petunia gum-paste cutter. Plump yellow stamens sit in the middle of the lotuslike faux daisy petals. The pinched apex of each petal also reminds me of the pure white pointed marble cupola of a mosque. I love finding the shape of a tiny flower petal echoed in a monumental work of architecture. I encourage you to invent your own flowers; they're fun to make.

DIRECTIONS:

1. On a smooth surface, roll out a thin sheet of sugar paste.
2. Punch out a series of flowers with the cutter.
3. Gently pinch the apex of each petal between your thumb and middle finger.
4. Place the faux daisies onto your cake.
5. Pipe a big pearl of yellow royal icing in the center of the flower.

Finishing with Gold Dust, Pearl Dust, and Gold Leaf

This is perhaps my favorite part. When Dr. Frankenstein flipped the switch, his monster came to life. That's how I feel about gold dust and pearl dust—it's like switching on the cake lights. I gild the swags, the roping, and the tassels; I paint the pearls and the filigree with an iridescent finish; then I turn down the studio lights so they're just bright enough to illuminate the gold and pearl. And the cake comes to life.

DIRECTIONS:
Gold Dust

1. Sprinkle about ¼ teaspoon of gold dust into a tea saucer.
2. Add about ⅛ teaspoon of lemon extract to the dust. Mix it into a thin paste.
3. Apply the paste to decorations with a small paintbrush.

DIRECTIONS:
Pearl Dust

1. Sprinkle a small amount of pearl dust into a tea saucer.
2. Add an even smaller amount of lemon extract to the dust. Mix it into a thin shiny paste.
3. Apply the paste to decorations with a small paintbrush.

Take the white of an egge being beaten to a froth . . . . With a Conies tailes end moisted a little, take the gold by the corner, lay it on the place, being first made moist, and with another taile of a Cony dry, presse the gold down close . . . . It will sticke to it . . . . Skew or brush off the gold with the foote of a Hare or Cony.

—Stuart Peachey, *Cooking Techniques and Equipment, 1580–1660* (1994)

DIRECTIONS:
Gold Leaf

1. Lightly beat one egg white until loosened up.
2. Using a small paintbrush, paint the desired shape or area with egg white.
3. With a separate, dry sable paintbrush, lift a piece of gold from its page and place it on the moistened area. With a larger sable brush, gently press it down. (You must do this in a still room.)
4. Using the same dry brush, carefully remove excess gold leaf.

NOTE: *This is a difficult skill; it must be practiced.*

CAKE TOPPERS

What should I put on top of the cake? Whether it's a wedding cake, a birthday cake, or a sugar sculpture, this is a serious design issue. The topper should be an integral part of the design, but it must also be the crowning element. In some cases the cake serves as the pedestal leading up to a spectacular sugar work. Why devote all that attention to detailing your cake, then top it off with something of lesser impact? There are many premade cake toppers on the market, but it's best to make your own. Sugar chalices and crowns are my personal trademark. I've made them for years, but they are difficult and time-consuming. So along with the chalices I am including some other options, which involve simply using some of the aforementioned motifs and techniques (such as pastillage curlicues and sugar-paste marbles) in a different context.

Margaret's Pastillage Chalices

My sugar chalices are inspired by chalices and reliquaries, as well as devotional objects I've seen in paintings, church basements, and museum treasuries. The base and knop of my chalices are sculpted by hand (the knop is the connecting ball between the two halves of the base), but the cup itself is made from a mold. A cake-decorating supplier will have plastic molds for molding chocolate. They work just as well with pastillage. However, I encourage you to look around your house (in the kitchen, on the mantel, or on your bedroom bureau) for a trivet, a cup, a bowl—some elegant shape, not too deep, which would serve as a mold for pastillage.

DIRECTIONS:

The Base

1. Roll out two separate plum-size balls of pastillage.
2. One at a time, place each ball onto your work surface and form it into a pedestal shape.
3. Set the pedestal shapes out to dry overnight on a baking sheet. Turn them upside down the next day and let them dry another two days.

The Knop

1. Shape one ball of pastillage the size of a large gumball.
2. Set it out to dry with the other two pieces.

The Cup

1. Make sure your mold is clean, dry, and dusted with cornstarch. Roll out a thin sheet of pastillage (the same thickness as used for curlicues) and carefully lay it into the mold.
2. With a paring knife, trim off any edges showing above the mold.
3. Let it set in the mold overnight. Then remove it from the mold, turn it cup-down, and set it to dry overnight again.

Assembly

1. Fill a pastry bag with royal icing.
2. Pipe approximately $1/2$ teaspoon of royal icing onto the top of the first pedestal and place the knop on it. Clean off any excess royal icing.
3. Pipe $1/2$ teaspoon of icing on top of the knop and place the second pedestal upside down on top of it.
4. Pipe $1/2$ teaspoon of royal icing on top of the pedestal and top it with the pastillage cup.
5. Decorate with swags, fleurs-de-lis, or as desired.

Cleopatra is sometimes depicted holding a pearl over a **chalice** as a gesture of ostentation, and in still lifes an overturned chalice symbolizes vanitas. Socrates was given his hemlock in a chalice, and in the Decameron, *Ghismonda was presented with a chalice bearing the heart of her lover. Its associations are more positive in Judeo-Christian symbology. An angel delivers bread and a chalice to Elijah to give him strength to continue in the desert. And as the vessel for wine in Holy Communion, the chalice represents redemption.*

Akbar's Mystery Vessel

The function of Akbar's Mystery Vessel (which tops "Akbar's Cake," page 140) is between Akbar and me. I'll just say that it lies somewhere between a genie bottle and a water pipe.

DIRECTIONS:

1. Roll out a 10-inch cord of sugar paste the width of a thick pencil. Back it up against a ruler to make it perfectly straight. Let it dry in a sheet on parchment for at least one whole day. It will dry into a pole.
2. Make two chalice cups, the shape and size of your choice (see "Margaret's Pastillage Chalices," page 81). Before drying them, poke a dime-sized hole at the base of one of the cups. Let them dry in the mold overnight and out of the mold for another night.
3. When both sugar cups are completely dry, "glue" them together at the open end with royal icing, creating a round ball. Let the hollow, round sugar vessel dry overnight.
4. Place the dried sugar pole into the hole of the vessel.
5. Paint and decorate as desired.

Sugar-Sculpted Topper for "Tassels Are Beautiful"

DIRECTIONS:
1. Follow the procedure for making the base in "Margaret's Pastillage Chalices" (see page 81) but make the pedestals larger and let them dry for at least a week.
2. Adhere the chalice to the top of the pedestal.

Crown for "Queen of Symmetry"

This crown differs from the crowns typically worn during the Middle Ages. The Symmetry Queen's crown is an archetypal crown, like the one worn by the Imperial Margarine Queen on television commercials. It is very difficult to make, so instead I will show you how to make an equally beautiful crown that's truer to the medieval style—more like the Jughead crown.

DIRECTIONS:

1. On a clean surface dusted with cornstarch, roll out an 8-inch-long by 2½-inch-high strip of pastillage (the same thickness as used for curlicues).
2. Using a sharp paring knife, cut an even sequence of upside-down "V" shapes out of the bottom end of the strip (see the flat strip in the photograph).
3. Gently lift the "crown strip" from your work surface, place it inside a 3-inch-diameter by at least 1-inch-high cookie cutter. Cut off any excess pastillage so that it fits inside perfectly. Finesse the points of the crown. Let it dry inside the cutter overnight.

Optional: Pipe two strings of royal icing pearls around the base of the crown. Pipe pearls on top of the points. Gild all pearls with gold dust (see page 79).

Doves

Doves are a symbol of love and constancy. A pair of doves is the chief emblem of Venus. Two doves facing each other refer to concord (the opposing virtue of discord). The dove of the ark became the symbol of good tidings and peace personified. Billing doves suggest the lovers' embrace.

DIRECTIONS:

1. Roll a large sugar-paste marble the size of a large gumball.
2. To make the head, pinch the top of the marble.
3. To make the tail, pinch the bottom of the marble.
4. Finesse the shape of the dove, then let it dry overnight.
5. Adhere the dove to the top of your cake and finish it with gold dust or pearl dust (see page 79).

If you do your work well, and spend time on your jobs,
and good colors, you will get such a reputation that a wealthy
person will come to compensate you for the poor one; and your standing will be so good
for using good colors that if a master is getting one ducat for a figure, you will
be offered two . . . . As the saying goes, good work, good pay.

—Cennino d'Andrea Cennini, *Il Libro Dell' Arte* (15th century)

Color

Many of my cakewalks include a search for locally produced food colorings. They are difficult to find in some countries and easy to find in others. I have a collection of them, and I love to experiment with some of the more unusual pigments. I use them to paint my sculptures and portraits, but I am careful about using them on cakes that will be eaten. A wide range of food colors is available at a cake-decorating supplier to supplement the basic colors at your local supermarket. Keep in mind that liquid food color is good for painting while gel, paste, and powder food colors are ideal for coloring icings.

I sometimes attain the perfect hue straight from a bottle of food coloring. But I prefer mixing my own colors. Painting with food coloring is similar to painting with watercolors.

Hue is the color itself. It could be red, green, blue, yellow, umber, fuchsia, or yellowy-reddish-orange—any specific color at all, as long as you stick a name on it.

Saturation is how much of that particular hue you have, or in watercolor terms the amount of water you mix with it. If you mix lots of water into that yellowy-reddish-orange hue, it will loose its intensity, its saturation. But it will still be an echo of the original color recipe.

Value is determined by the amount of white added to a particular hue. For example, picture a nice, saturated red. If a drop of white is added to it, it will no longer be red. It will be pink. When you add more white, it becomes an even lighter pink. Eventually, it will no longer red or even pink—it will be white.

Painting with Food Coloring

When I was growing up, there were two types of children: the ones who colored within the lines and the ones who couldn't, or wouldn't. The ones who could were good looking and had lots of friends; the ones who couldn't were omitted from kickball and forced to wear bad pants. It was hard for me to color inside the lines, but I got better at it. And my difficulty in staying in the lines never had any bearing on my ability to come up with good ideas. Ultimately, however, a steady hand is enormously useful in the realm of cake decorating, so this might be a good time to give it another try.

A word about airbrushing: Paint your cake—airbrushing is for T-shirts and vans.

DIRECTIONS:
1. Use good-quality brushes.
2. Try to stay in the lines.

CAKE PREPARATION AND ASSEMBLY

A Few Practical Words about Working in the Kitchen

It helps to know what you are getting yourself into before you approach a huge, complicated project. Along with the immeasurable joy of seeing your cake come to life, which includes eating as much of that delicious cake trim, ganache, buttercream, and icing as you want to, there's the other side to this reality. Sugar paste can crack, royal icing can harden before you're ready, gold dust can lack luster, and colors can fade right before your eyes. The clock will keep on ticking, and the party is in two hours. And on top of it all, you're sitting in the middle of a messy kitchen with a sink full of mixing bowls, and you're covered in chocolate. Here are a few tips that might help.

1. Sometimes a design crisis can be solved with a sponge and a mop. If your workspace is messy, it can distract and confuse you, so get away from the cake and clean the kitchen.

2. Delicate gestures with lightly damp, clammy rags will get you nowhere, so be aggressive or it will take you forever to clean up your work area. Wet a clean sponge or rag thoroughly, put the weight of your entire body onto your hands, and with sweeping gestures clean that table.

3. Always keep your bench scraper by your side, and a trash basket at your disposal.

4. Don't decorate your cake in haste, but try to develop a rhythm and set goals for completion. For instance: "I will begin gilding the swags by three o'clock." You may not make the deadline, but that's okay—just thinking about it will have started you thinking about the next step. Stay a step ahead of yourself.

5. Drink lots of water, and take a stretch.

Your life should always be arranged just as if you were studying theology, or philosophy, or other theories, that is to say, eating and drinking moderately, at least twice a day, electing digestible and wholesome dishes, and light wines; saving and sparing your hand, preserving it from such strains as heaving stones, crowbar, and many other things which are bad for your hand.

—Cennino d'Andrea Cennini,
Il Libro dell' Arte (15th century)

How to Slice and Fill a Cake

Place the cake onto a cardboard disk of the same size (see "Tools and Ingredients," page 214). Before slicing it into layers, it must cool. Ideally, it should be refrigerated overnight. Since I make most of my cakes with ganache, I've used it in this example.

TOOLS AND INGREDIENTS:
Serrated knife; cardboard disks the same diameter as your cake; filling of choice; standing kitchen mixer; metal spatula

DIRECTIONS:

1. Slice the cake into layers about $1/2$-inch thick. Place each of them onto a cardboard disk of the proper size.

   Slicing takes practice. You may think you're cutting straight across, and suddenly the tip of your knife pops through the middle of the cake. To help prevent this from happening, you can get a sense of where the knife is by keeping a firm flat hand on the top of the cake (see photographs 1 and 2). (Be careful not to cut yourself.)

2. Fill the cake layers.

   Ganache is fickle. Temperature is everything. I turn my head for one second and it's gone from soupy to solid. If my kitchen is too cool, the ganache may seize up very quickly, making it impossible to spread onto cake layers. If my kitchen is too warm, it will be soupy, and spill off the sides of the cake. You can prevent these mood swings by implementing a few precautions.

WARM KITCHEN: Reserve some ganache in a metal bowl and put it in the fridge. Add to soupy ganache as needed.

COOL KITCHEN: Reserve some ganache in a metal bowl and place it on a simmering, not boiling, double boiler. Or place the reserved ganache in a glass bowl and warm in the microwave. Add to solid ganache as needed.

3. In a standing mixer with the paddle attachment, mix the ganache on low speed until it has a little bit of body.

4. With a metal spatula, spread about $1/4$ inch of ganache on the bottom cake layer (photograph 3). Place the second layer on top and gently pat it down with cardboard disk (photograph 4) to make it level and to be sure that it adheres to the layer of ganache beneath it, then spread a $1/4$ inch of ganache on it. Repeat until finished.

5. Now that the cake is filled, it's time to shape it. Use an offset serrated knife to trim it to desired shape and size. Make sure the edges are left clean and smooth (photograph 5).

How to Sculpt the Tiers of a Cake

TOOLS AND INGREDIENTS:

Serrated knife; cardboard template (optional); offset serrated knife

DIRECTIONS:

1. Before you begin carving the cake into shapes, make sure it's chilled through and through. This could mean a good hour and a half in the refrigerator, depending on its temperature.
2. Cut out a cardboard template of the shape you'd like the cake to be and place it on top of the filled and chilled cake. Position an offset serrated knife perpendicular to the template and cut the cake to the shape of the template. Or skip the template and, with the offet serrated knife, shape it by eye.

How to Ice a Cake

Oddly enough, I wrote this description at my favorite café while watching a herd of construction workers lay down a cement sidewalk with tremendous dexterity and grace. I realized how similar it was to icing a cake. I was so impressed.

Icing fills in the gaps, seals up the cake, and smoothes the surface in preparation for the official icing (marzipan or sugar paste). The cake edges must be clean and smooth before you apply the final icing. Like delicious joint compound or glue, this is the icing on the cake before the icing of the cake.

TOOLS AND INGREDIENTS:

Turntable; icing; spatula

DIRECTIONS:

1. Place the cake in the center of the turntable.
2. Place a hefty amount of icing in the center of the cake (see photograph 1).
3. With a spatula, spread out icing just beyond the edge of the cake while spinning the turntable counterclockwise (photograph 2).
4. Build up the sides one area at a time (be generous—you can always remove excess icing later) until the cake is completely iced. It should have a creamy, delicious, homemade look (photograph 3).
5. Hold the spatula in place and spin the turntable counterclockwise while smoothing down the top of the cake. Let excess go beyond the edge. When you're done, return excess icing to the mixing bowl.
6. With the spatula held in place exactly perpendicular to the turntable, spin the cake again and smooth down the sides. Continue spinning until the cake is neatly iced (photograph 4).
7. To finish, place the spatula at one end of the cake, and glide it towards you, across the cake, until the top is nice and smooth (photograph 5).

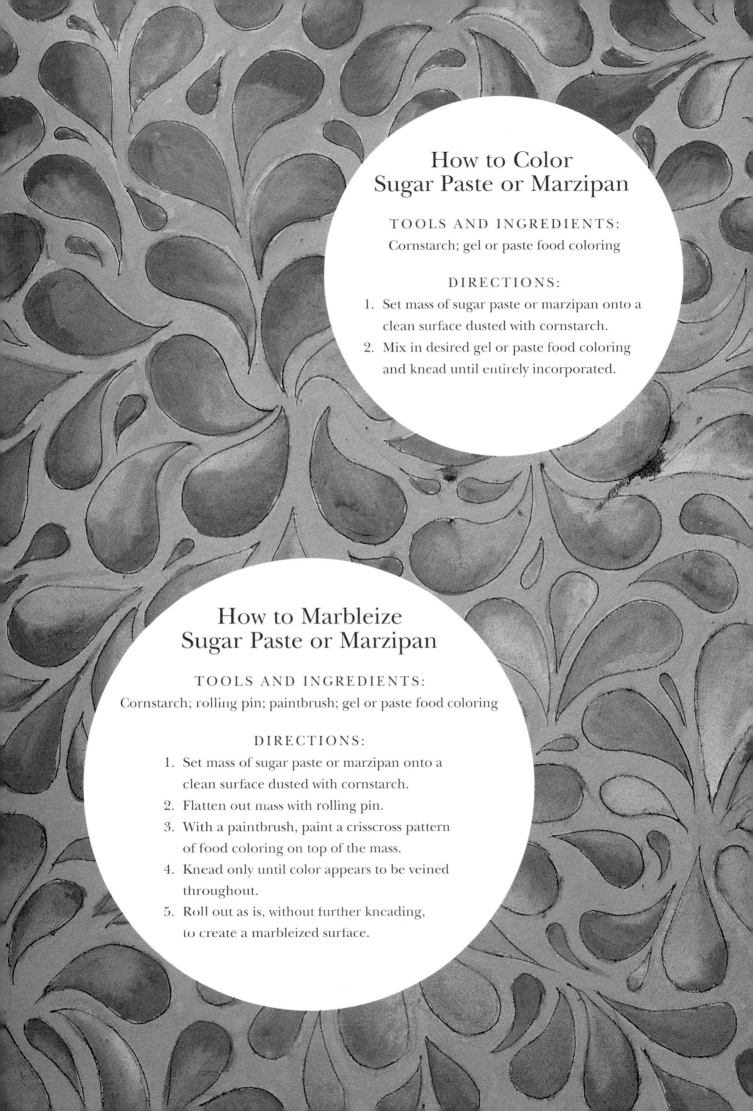

How to Color
Sugar Paste or Marzipan

TOOLS AND INGREDIENTS:
Cornstarch; gel or paste food coloring

DIRECTIONS:

1. Set mass of sugar paste or marzipan onto a clean surface dusted with cornstarch.
2. Mix in desired gel or paste food coloring and knead until entirely incorporated.

How to Marbleize
Sugar Paste or Marzipan

TOOLS AND INGREDIENTS:
Cornstarch; rolling pin; paintbrush; gel or paste food coloring

DIRECTIONS:

1. Set mass of sugar paste or marzipan onto a clean surface dusted with cornstarch.
2. Flatten out mass with rolling pin.
3. With a paintbrush, paint a crisscross pattern of food coloring on top of the mass.
4. Knead only until color appears to be veined throughout.
5. Roll out as is, without further kneading, to create a marbleized surface.

How to Cover Cakes
with Sugar Paste or Marzipan

As soon as I've determined the shape of the cake, I clean my work surface and prepare to cover it in either sugar paste or marzipan. When that's done, I see the blank canvas and get very excited. This is when I make my royal icing (see page 201), which takes about five minutes or so; just enough time away from the undecorated cake so I can reapproach it with a fresh eye. (NOTE: *You need to cover each layer of your cake separately.*)

TOOLS AND INGREDIENTS:
Cornstarch; rolling pin; paring knife; icing smoother

This table will help you figure out how much sugar paste or marzipan is required.

FOR A:	YOU'LL NEED:	FOR A:	YOU'LL NEED:
4-inch cake	$1/2$ pound	14-inch cake	$2\,3/4$ pounds
6-inch cake	$3/4$ pound	16-inch cake	$3\,2/3$ pounds
8-inch cake	1 pound	18-inch cake	$4\,1/2$ pounds
10-inch cake	$1\,1/4$ pounds	20-inch cake	5 pounds
12-inch cake	$2\,1/4$ pounds		

DIRECTIONS:

1. Dust a clean smooth surface with cornstarch. Knead your sugar paste or marzipan into a pliable mass (see photographs 1 and 2).

2. Roll out the sugar paste (often called rolled fondant) or marzipan to a sheet between $1/4$ to $1/8$ inch thick, turning it by 90 degrees midway through rolling to even it out. Continue rolling until your sheet measures at least 2 inches beyond the size of your cake layer (this measurement must include the sides.) From time to time, gently slide a spatula beneath the sugar paste to be sure it's not sticking (photograph 3).

3. Roll the sugar paste back onto the rolling pin, then carefully unroll it onto the cake. Quickly smooth out the top and sides and adhere it to the cake. There will be overlapping along the bottom edge. Smooth it out by lifting and tucking where necessary. This takes practice (photographs 4 to 6).

4. Trim the edges with a paring knife. It's always better to trim off too little than too much (photograph 7).

5. Smooth the surface with an icing smoother (photograph 8).

How to Assemble a Multi-Tiered Cake

A cake, like a building, has a structure of flat planes and girders hidden within the cake to keep it from collapsing. This structure can't be fooled with.

This is for a five-tiered cake consisting of 12-inch, 10-inch, 8-inch, 6-inch, and 4-inch round layers. Each should already be iced and covered with sugar paste or marzipan. Adjust the directions for cakes of other sizes.

TOOLS AND INGREDIENTS:

One 16-inch cake base; 10-inch, 8-inch, 6-inch, and 4-inch plastic separator plates; plastic or wooden dowels; pencil; a serrated knife or pruning shears; royal icing (see page 201)

(NOTE: *The separator plates must always match the exact size of the cakes that will rest on them.*)

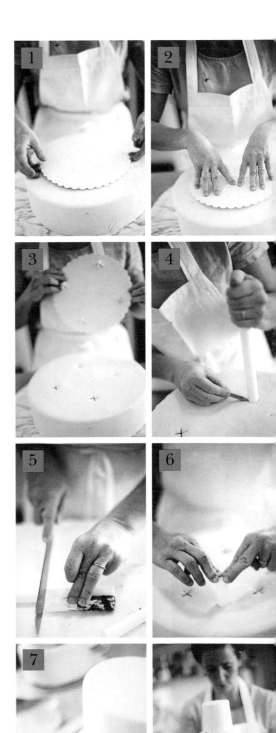

DIRECTIONS:

1. Place the 12-inch cake in the center of the cake base.
2. Place the 10-inch plastic separator plate precisely in the middle of the 12-inch cake. Make an imprint of the plate by gently pressing the plate into the cake. Remove the separator plate (see photographs 1 to 3).
3. Find a point halfway between the marks left by two adjoining feet on the separator plate. Insert a dowel into the cake at that point about 1 inch inside the encircled area (photograph 4). Make sure the dowel is vertical.
4. With the pencil, mark the exact level of the icing on the exposed end of the dowel. Remove the dowel (photograph 4).
5. With the serrated knife or pruning shears, cut the dowel at the mark (photograph 5).
6. Cut the three remaining dowels to the exact size of the first one.
7. Place one of the cut dowels back in the "measuring" hole (photograph 6). Call that 12 o'clock and place the other dowels at 3 o'clock, 6 o'clock, and 9 o'clock. Be sure to insert them vertically. Position them 1 inch inside the edge of the area you marked with the separator plate.
8. Pipe a tablespoon of royal icing in the center of the cake and replace the 10-inch separator plate in its position on top of the cake.
9. Place the 10-inch cake on top of the plate (photograph 7).
10. Repeat the same process with the remaining cakes.

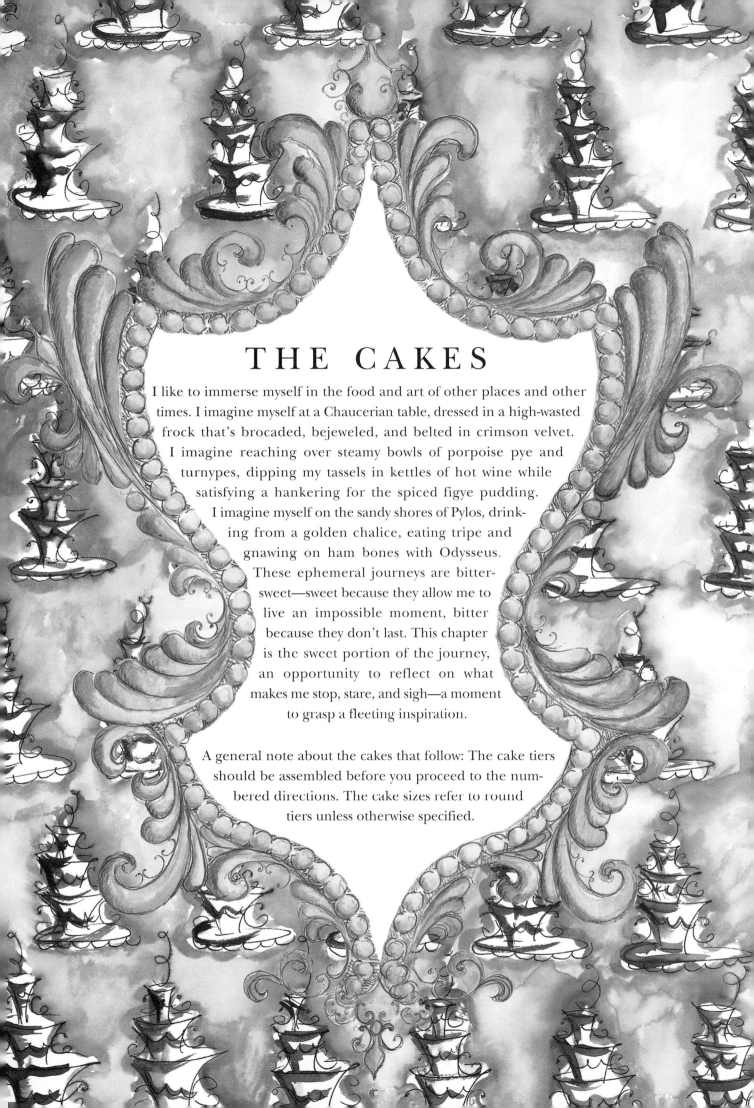

THE CAKES

I like to immerse myself in the food and art of other places and other times. I imagine myself at a Chaucerian table, dressed in a high-wasted frock that's brocaded, bejeweled, and belted in crimson velvet. I imagine reaching over steamy bowls of porpoise pye and turnypes, dipping my tassels in kettles of hot wine while satisfying a hankering for the spiced figye pudding. I imagine myself on the sandy shores of Pylos, drinking from a golden chalice, eating tripe and gnawing on ham bones with Odysseus. These ephemeral journeys are bittersweet—sweet because they allow me to live an impossible moment, bitter because they don't last. This chapter is the sweet portion of the journey, an opportunity to reflect on what makes me stop, stare, and sigh—a moment to grasp a fleeting inspiration.

A general note about the cakes that follow: The cake tiers should be assembled before you proceed to the numbered directions. The cake sizes refer to round tiers unless otherwise specified.

When in Doubt— Polka Dots

Let's start small and simple. This cake is easy to make and doesn't call for complicated piping. Instead it requires a good eye for color and placement. For colors I chose orange and white, but you might want to pick your own.

CAKE SIZES:
8-inch, 6-inch, and 4-inch tiers; all 3½ inches high

MOTIFS AND TECHNIQUES:
Polka dots; sugar-paste marbles; finishing with pearl dust

TOOLS AND INGREDIENTS:
Orange sugar paste; white sugar paste; paintbrush; pearl dust finish; glass of water

DIRECTIONS:
1. Cover the cakes with the orange sugar paste.
2. Choose the placement for the polka dots and mark the spots with a moist paintbrush. Then adhere the white polka dots to your cake.
3. Pile some sugar-paste marbles on the top tier.
4. Place a few marbles along the edges of the remaining tiers.
5. Finish polka dots and sugar paste marbles with pearl dust.

Faux Daisy
Basket Weave

This is a very pretty cake with a straightforward design, but beneath the surface there is a layer of marzipan to give it a little more aesthetic weight.

TOOLS AND INGREDIENTS:

Marzipan or sugar paste; pastry bag; #47 basket-weave tip; #7 round tip; yellow royal icing; small rolling pin; pastillage; petunia gum-paste cutter or another cutter of choice; pearl dust finish; paintbrush

DIRECTIONS:

1. Cover the cakes with the marzipan or sugar paste.
2. Pipe the basket-weave pattern onto the cakes with the yellow icing and the basket-weave tip.
3. Roll out the pastillage, cut out faux daisies and finish them with pearl dust. Place them along the ledges of the cake and pipe a yellow stamen into the middle of each with the round tip.
4. Make some curlicues and attach them with royal icing to the top tier of the cake.
5. Attach a few daisies to the curlicue topper with royal icing.

MOTIFS AND TECHNIQUES:

Basket weave; faux daisies; finishing with pearl dust; pastillage curlicues

CAKE SIZES:

10-inch, 8-inch, and 6-inch tiers; all $3^{1}/_{2}$ inches high

Decal Recall

I must have been four or five when
a crazy bunch of flowers mysteriously appeared in
our bathtub in Levittown. They were rubber decals in fabulous pink, orange, purple, green, and yellow. I recall feeling the
gritty, rubbery texture on the soles of my feet, and my fascination with
the fact that not only did they look great but they were designed for
safety. This was an early lesson in form following function and a smart way
to get me into the tub. Mother knew. This comic flora has been with me
ever since, and I've drawn it everywhere, from paper to walls to tables to
cakes. No matter how many times I make this cake, I never get tired of
it. Of course, it changes each time I make it. This cake requires a bit
of drawing—right onto the cake. But it's fairly quick and easy,
and it always looks fresh and good. You could also cover this
cake with marzipan. If you're interested, see the
Marzipan recipe, page 199).

CAKE SIZES:
14-inch, 12-inch,
10-inch, 8-inch,
6-inch, and 4-inch
sculpted tiers;
all 3$\frac{1}{2}$ inches high

DIRECTIONS:

1. Cover the cakes with sugar paste.
2. Choose your colors and sketch the flowers onto the cake surface with a paintbrush dipped in the color you have chosen for the petals. (See the image on this page for to-scale example.)
3. Paint color onto the petals first, then the stamens. Do the background color last.
4. Attach the #6 round tip to a pastry bag filled with royal icing. Pipe a pearl border around the bottom edge of the cakes.
5. Fill the cornetta with royal icing and pipe small royal icing pearls around the periphery of the petals. When the icing is dry, finish the pearl borders with pearl dust and gild the pearl beading with gold dust.
6. Adhere an arrangement of sugar paste marbles and curlicues to the top tier, and attach a few faux daisies to the curlicues.

TOOLS AND
INGREDIENTS:
Sugar paste; paintbrushes;
food coloring; pastry bag;
#6 round tip; royal icing;
paper cornetta; pearl dust
and gold dust finishes

MOTIFS AND
TECHNIQUES:
Painting with food coloring;
royal icing pearls; finishing with
pearl dust and gold dust;
sugar paste marbles; pastillage
curlicues; faux daisies

Afternoon with Frederick

tea House   (green)

Palace   (yellow)

I have entitled this cake "Afternoon with Frederick" because had Frederick the Great (the former king of Prussia) been alive during my visit to the Sans Souci Palace in Potsdam, Germany, I would have invited myself for afternoon tea.

A wooded path opens to the sunny clearing to Frederick's Tea House, an enclosed gazebolike structure of sage green and white. A flute is playing—it's Frederick himself, and he invites me in. My impromptu visit warrants my very special gift. He eyes me quizzically upon receiving my yellow and white cake. I quickly explain, "Oh, no, dear Frederick, the reasoning behind this yellow and white cake is to honor your splendid yellow and white palace over there on top of the hill, and to contrast with the green and white tea house in which we sit." He is enlightened. We have tea and cake. He gives me a lesson. It's an agreeable afternoon.

CAKE SIZES:
12-inch, 10-inch,
8-inch, 6-inch,
and 4-inch tiers;
all 4 inches high

MOTIFS AND TECHNIQUES:
Grapes; royal icing pearls;
royal icing flourishes;
pastillage curlicues;
finishing with pearl dust

TOOLS AND INGREDIENTS:
Yellow marzipan or another
color of choice; pastry bag;
#4 round tip; royal icing; paper
cornetta; pearl dust finish;
paintbrush

DIRECTIONS:

1. Cover the cakes with the yellow marzipan.

2. Attach the #4 tip to a pastry bag filled with royal icing and pipe a pearl border around the tier.

3. With the same tip, pipe grapes directly onto the cake. (Don't forget the leaves.) Or make the grapes ahead and attach them to the cake with royal icing.

4. Fill a paper cornetta with royal icing. Cut a small hole at the tip and pipe royal icing flourishes in the empty spaces.

5. Attach pastillage curlicues to the sides with royal icing.

6. Finish the grapes in pearl dust.

7. Attach a curlicue topper.

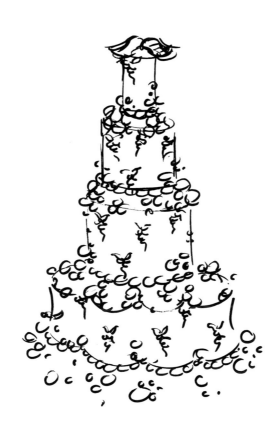

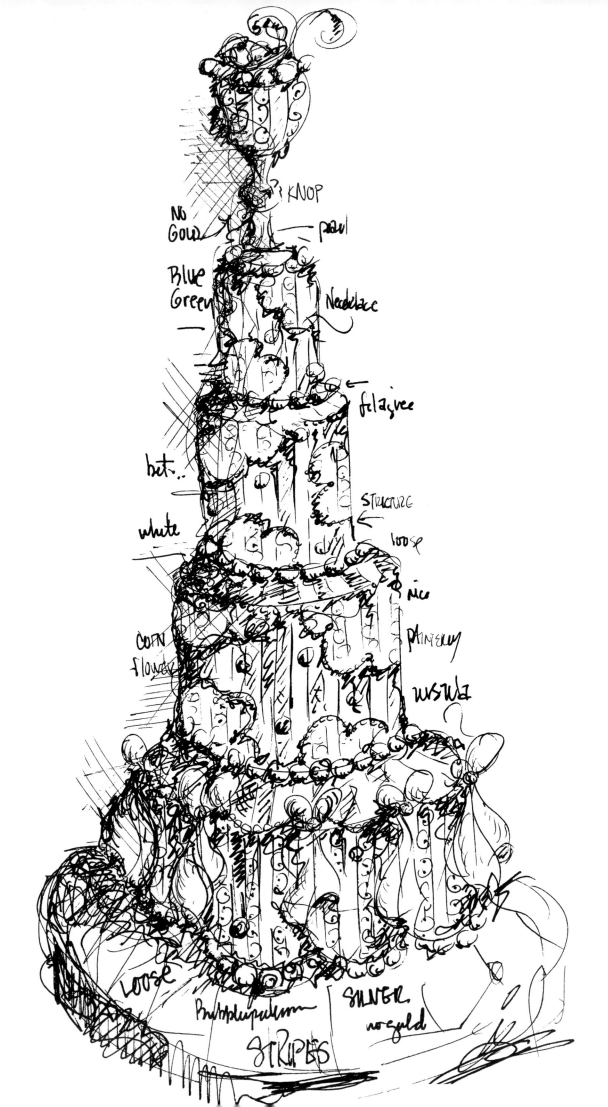

Stripes Are Nice

I never see stripes without thinking of my friend Leslie, who spent five years of her life in the Lower East Side of Manhattan, rummaging through old boxes of strange and beautiful ribbon. She'd haggle down the price with the Hasidic salesmen, return to her Brooklyn studio, and proceed to glue ribbon in stripes onto plywood.

From afar, each stripe painting appears sharp, stylish, and confident. But when you see them up close, glue seeps out from beneath the stripes, and fingerprints stain the satin finish. They become vulnerable and their secrets leak out from beneath their shiny surfaces. Each striped piece tells its own story and is quite beautiful.

I made my stripe cake during my periwinkle and celadon phase. I wanted the stripes to look neat and orderly from across the room but loose and painterly up close. By breaking up the design with polka dots and piping, and finishing the cake with a curlicue topper, I hoped to call attention to the stripes.

CAKE SIZES:
18-inch beveled tier;
14-inch, 12-inch, 10-inch,
8-inch, and 6-inch round
tiers; all 4 inches high

TOOLS AND INGREDIENTS:
Sugar paste; periwinkle and
celadon food coloring; metal ruler;
paintbrushes; silver dust and
pearl dust finishes; pastry bag;
#3 round tip; #5 round tip;
royal icing; paper cornetta

MOTIFS AND TECHNIQUES:
Painting with food coloring;
piping with royal icing; polka dots
royal icing pearls; pastillage
Ursulines; sugar-paste roping;
sugar-paste tassels; chalice topper;
curlicues; finishing with pearl
dust and silver dust

DIRECTIONS:

1. Cover the cakes with the sugar paste.
2. Prepare the colors.
3. Place a metal ruler against the side of the cake and begin painting vertical stripes in alternating colors. You can vary the width of the stripes as long as they remain parallel. Wipe down the ruler to remove excess food coloring after each stripe.
4. Paint silver-dust lines in between the stripes. (Edible silver dust , available at cake-decorating suppliers, is applied in the same method as gold dust.) Use the ruler.
5. Attach the #3 round tip to a pastry bag filled with royal icing. Pipe a pearl necklace "bubble" design onto the tiers.
6. Using a cornetta, pipe royal icing designs as desired inside pearl necklace bubbles.
7. Adhere polka dots between the bubbles.
8. Attach the #5 round tip to the pastry bag and pipe a pearl border along the cake tiers.
9. Adhere pastillage Ursulines between the bevels on the bottom tier.
10. Adhere sugar-paste roping to the first, third, and sixth tiers.
11. Attach a silver tassel to the end of the sugar-paste roping.
12. Adhere a chalice topper and pastillage curlicues on the top of the cake.
13. Finish all piping with pearl dust.
14. Gild the roping and tassels with silver dust.

It's All About the Bows

This cake was originally designed to match an ecru and white satin wedding dress. I have since played with the colors. It is a simple, elegant design, but only if you remember—it's all about the bows.

MOTIFS AND TECHNIQUES:
Painting with food coloring; royal icing pearls; pastillage bows; finishing with pearl dust

CAKE SIZES:
8-inch, 6-inch, 4-inch, and 2-inch tiers; all 4 inches high

TOOLS AND INGREDIENTS:
Sugar paste; food coloring; paintbrush; pastry bag; #5 round tip; royal icing; rolling pin; pastillage; pearl dust finish

DIRECTIONS:

1. Cover the cakes with the sugar paste.
2. Paint the lower two inches of each tier with the color of your choice.
3. Attach a #5 round tip to a pastry bag filled with royal icing. Pipe a pearl border along the base of each tier and another pearl border parallel to it halfway up, at the edge of the painted area of each tier.
4. Roll out the pastillage and create four bows in graduated sizes.
5. Once the bows are completely dry, pipe royal icing onto the back of each bow and adhere it to the cake. Hold it in place for a minute or so to let it set.
6. Finish bows and top half of each tier with pearl dust.

Homage
to Linoleum

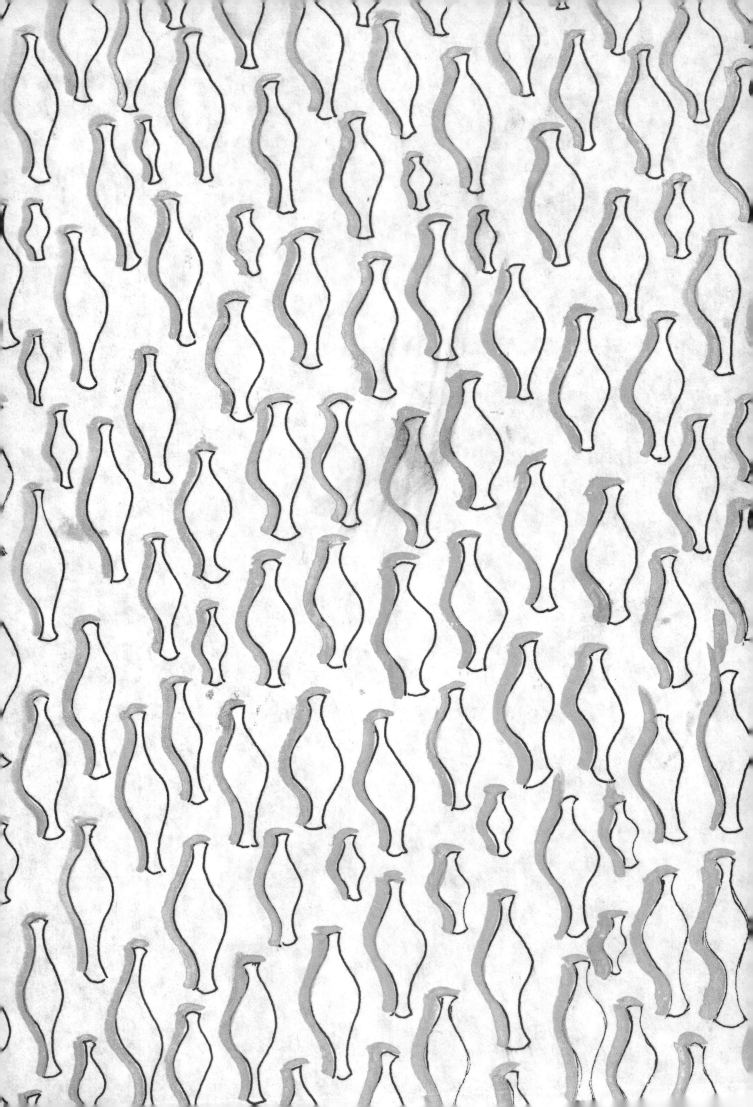

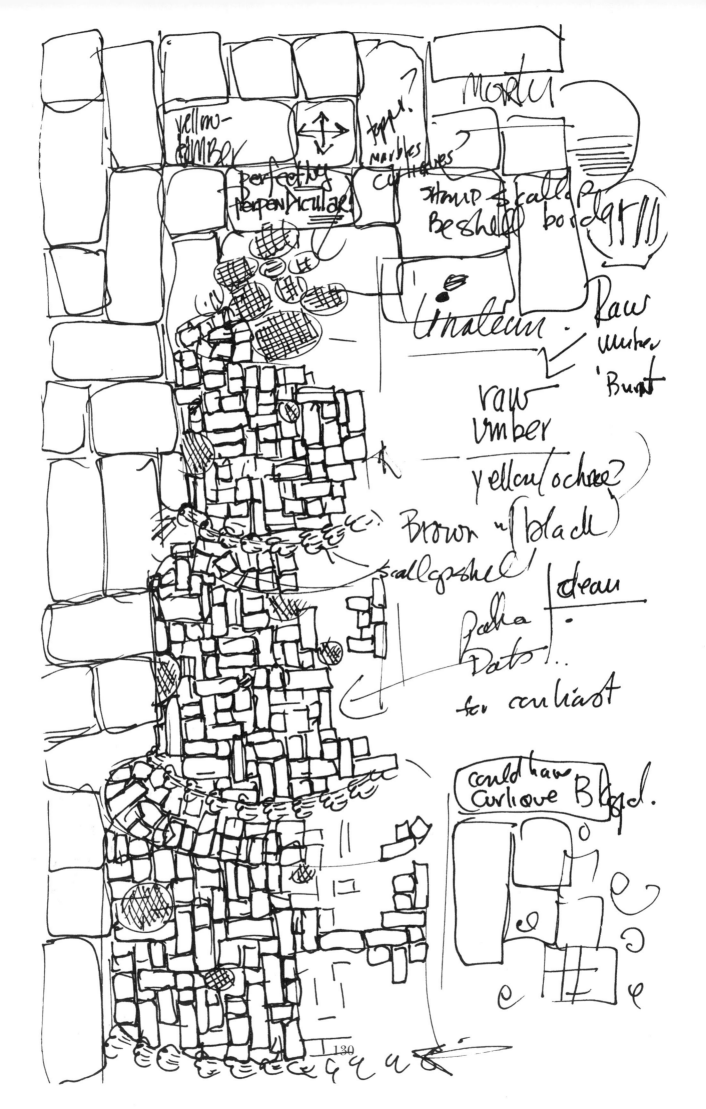

Mortar

yellow-umber?

perfectly perpendicular?

apps? marbles curtiques?

thiny scallops
Be shell border

Linoleum.

Raw umber 'Burnt

raw umber

yellow ochre?

Brown n[black]

scallopshell

clean

Pale Pats!..

for contrast

could have Curlique B[?]

After the introduction, do I need to say more about linoleum? I can say two more things. The interlocking rectangles and squares of this linoleum pattern remind me of a silent but chaotic traffic jam. And I think the rounded polka dots look like traffic lights.

DIRECTIONS:
1. Cover the cakes with the sugar paste.
2. Paint the linoleum pattern onto the entire cake, keeping the lines strictly perpendicular. You can do this by eye, but an easier (though no less time-consuming) method is to use a metal ruler to delineate the pattern first, and to paint in the squares and rectangles second. If you use a ruler, wipe it down often.
3. Attach the #18 shell tip to a pastry bag filled with royal icing. Pipe an even scallop-shell border around the base of the tiers.
4. Apply a few polka dots to the linoleum surface.

Crowning Moments
1. Adhere pastillage curlicues and a few sugar-paste marbles to the top of the cake.
2. When the royal icing is dry, finish the scallop shells, polka dots, and curlicues with pearl dust.

TOOLS AND INGREDIENTS:
Sugar paste; metal ruler (optional); food coloring; small paintbrush; pastry bag; #18 shell tip; royal icing; pearl dust finish

CAKE SIZES:
10-inch, 8-inch, 6-inch, and 4-inch tiers; all 4 inches high

MOTIFS AND TECHNIQUES:
Painting with food coloring; scallop shells; polka dots (optional); pastillage curlicues; sugar-paste marbles; finishing with pearl dust

Sidral
Bragulat
GUST TUTTI-FRUTTI
Preparat per: Andrés Montón, S.A.
C/. Barcelona, 43 - La Llagosta
Pes Net: 16 grs

Gust Tutti-Frutti

I can't persuade marzipan
to taste like lemons, or limes,
or sweet juicy oranges, but
I can make the most of their
brilliant shapes and colors by
putting these great-looking
little 3-D chunks of color onto
a cake. Because it's difficult
to adhere them to the sides of
the cake, I filled in the empty
spaces there with some royal
icing grapes and fleurs-de-lis.

CAKE SIZES:
10-inch beveled tier;
8-inch, 6-inch, and
4-inch round tiers;
all 4 inches high

**TOOLS AND
INGREDIENTS:**
Sugar paste; orange, lemon, and
lime-green marzipan; pastry bag;
#4 round tip; royal icing;
gold dust and pearl dust finishes;
paper cornetta

**MOTIFS AND
TECHNIQUES:**
Marzipan fruits; swags; royal icing
grapes; royal icing flourishes;
finishing with gold dust and
pearl dust; sugar doves topper

DIRECTIONS:
1. Cover the cakes with the sugar paste.
2. Adhere marzipan fruits along the ledges of the tiers with royal icing.
3. Attach the #4 round tip to a pastry bag filled with royal icing. Pipe swags on the tiers.
4. Pipe royal icing grapes (and leaves) along the ledges of the tiers.
5. Fill the cornetta with royal icing and pipe flourishes beneath the swags.
6. Finish the grapes with pearl dust, and gild their leaves and the swags with gold dust.

Crowning Moment
1. Attach two sugar doves to the top.

Akbar's Cake

In 1556, at the age of fourteen,

Akbar inherited the throne of India,

a Hindu nation. He was a Muslim

and yet his religious tolerance

strengthened his empire and earned

him the title Akbar the Great.

Akbar's interest in merging the

decorative elements of Persian

painting, the dynamism of

Indian painting, and eventually

the realism of European painting

culminated in the magnificent

artworks of the Mughal dynasty.

CAKE SIZES:
12-inch,
8-inch,
6-inch,
and 4-inch
sculpted tiers;
all 4 inches
high

MOTIFS AND TECHNIQUES:
Painting with
food coloring;
royal icing pearls;
filigree; sugar-paste
roping; pastillage
paisleys; Akbar's
Mystery Vessel;
finishing with gold
dust and pearl dust

TOOLS AND INGREDIENTS:
Marzipan; red, blue,
and yellow food
coloring; paintbrush; rolling
pin; small petunia and small
poinsettia gum-paste cutters
or other flower cutters of
choice; pastillage; pastry
bag; #4 round tip; royal
icing; gold dust and pearl
dust finishes

DIRECTIONS:
1. Cover the cakes with marzipan.

First Tier
1. Paint the side of the tier in red and the top ledge in yellow.
2. On a clean surface, roll out a thin sheet of marzipan. Cut out small flowers with the petunia cutter. Cover the remaining marzipan with plastic wrap and set aside. Adhere the flowers to the tier and paint them blue.
3. Attach the #4 round tip to a pastry bag filled with royal icing. Pipe pearls between and in the middle of each flower. Pipe smaller pearls at the point of each flower petal.
4. With the #4 tip, pipe a pearl border around the tier and smaller pearls along the top rim.
5. Roll out sugar-paste roping and drape it along the points of the tier.

Second Tier
1. Paint the side of the tier in blue and the top in red.
2. Uncover the marzipan and cut out flower shapes with the poinsettia (or small diamond-shape) cutter. Cover the remaining marzipan with plastic wrap and set aside. Adhere the flowers to the tier and paint them yellow.
3. Pipe royal icing pearls between and in the middle of each shape. Decorate each one with royal icing flourishes.
4. Pipe a pearl border around the base of the tier and a smaller pearl border along the top rim.

Third Tier
1. Paint the side of the tier in yellow and the top in red.
2. Pipe royal icing flourishes all over the tier.
3. Pipe a pearl border along the base of the tier and a smaller pearl border along the top rim.
4. Drape sugar-paste roping from the points of the tier.

Fourth Tier
1. Paint the side of the tier in blue and the top in red.
2. Uncover the marzipan and cut out flower shapes with the poinsettia (or small diamond-shape) cutter. Cover the remaining marzipan with plastic wrap and set aside. Adhere the flowers to the tier and paint them yellow.
3. Pipe royal icing pearls between and in the middle of each shape. Decorate each one with royal icing flourishes.
4. Pipe a pearl border around the base of the tier and a smaller pearl border along the top rim.

Crowning Moments
1. Attach large pastillage paisleys to the sides of the cake with royal icing, and attach small pastillage paisleys along the dips in the rim of the top tier.
2. Pipe small pearls along the border of the large paisleys.
3. Adhere Akbar's Mystery Vessel to the top tier with royal icing.
4. Attach small pastillage teardrops (pre-paisley shapes) between the sugar-paste roping on the third tier.
5. Finish the sugar-paste roping, royal icing flourishes, paisleys, and teardrops with gold dust.
6. Finish the pearl borders and other pearls with pearl dust.

The lotus-flower-shaped tiers of this cake—painted with baked

reds, curry-paste oranges, buttery saffrons, and ethereal lapis blues

that evoke illuminated manuscripts—are embroidered with icing

arabesques and paisley pirouettes. Garland necklaces of gold loop from

the tiers, which are buttressed by gold paisleys. Had Akbar invited

me to lunch at his palace, I would have brought him this cake as a gift.

I painted the flower patterns on this cake by hand, but you can cut out the

flower shapes with a gum-paste cutter and apply them to the cake.

Purple Makes the Best Winding Robe

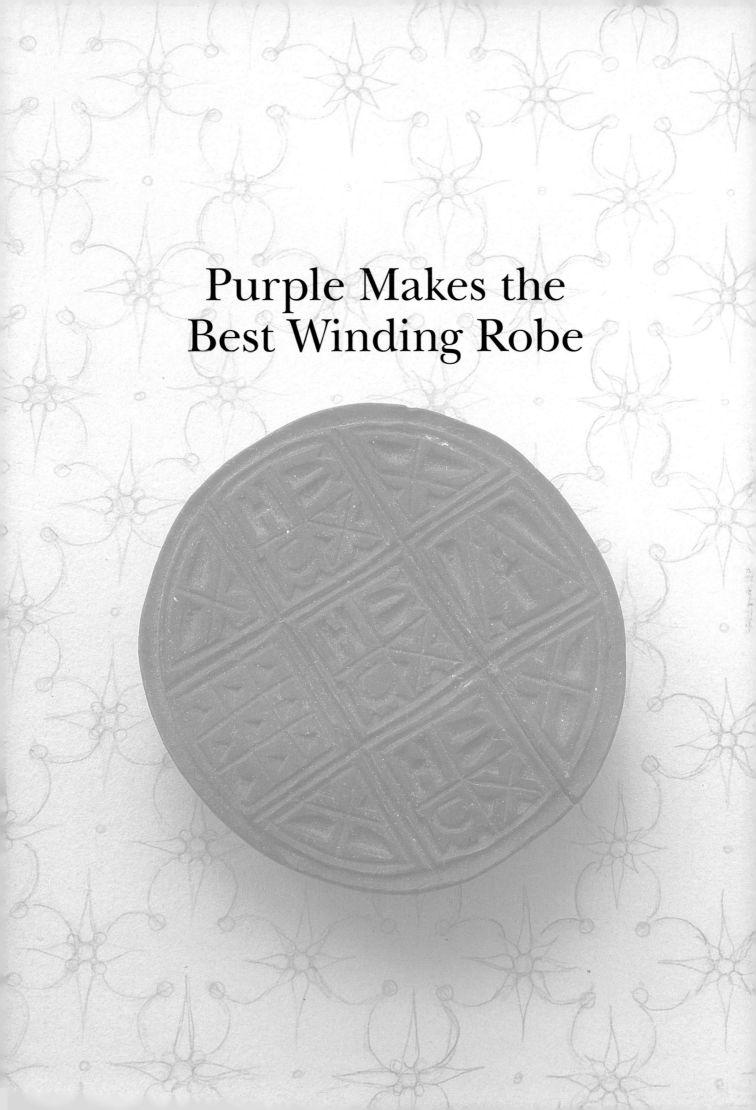

A mosaic panel at San Vitale in Ravenna, Italy, depicts Emperor Justinian in his purple chlamys, a magnificent winding robe. The chlamys was the official garb of Justinian and his wife, Empress Theodora.

I cut out all my tiles by hand. You can do that or you can use gum-paste cutters. Before you begin decorating the cake, plan your mosaic. You can do this by designing the pattern on a sheet of paper, using the different shapes of the gum-paste cutters. This is a good time to choose your colors, too.

CAKE SIZES:
12-inch beveled tier; 10-inch sculpted tier; 8-inch and 6-inch round tiers; all 4 inches high

TOOLS AND INGREDIENTS:
Marzipan; large paintbrush; simple syrup; sugar paste; cornstarch; small rolling pin; assorted gum-paste cutters *or* butter knife; purple, yellow, and brown food coloring; paintbrush; pastry bag; #4 round tip; royal icing; pastillage; gold dust finish

MOTIFS AND TECHNIQUES:
Sugar mosaic; painting with food coloring; sugar-paste roping; royal icing pearls; finishing with gold dust; purple pastillage Ursuline; chalice topper

DIRECTIONS:
1. Cover the cakes with a thin layer of marzipan.
2. Moisten marzipan covered cakes with a large paintbrush dipped in simple syrup.
3. Coat the marzipan-covered cakes with sugar paste.
4. To form the *tesserae* (the individual tiles of the mosaic), dust a smooth, clean work surface with cornstarch and roll out the sugar paste. Press the paste with a gum-paste cutter or a butter knife just enough to leave a crease.
5. When you have marked your design into the cake, fill in the creases with royal icing "mortar" of the desired color. Remove excess mortar.
6. Paint each tile its desired color.
7. Attach sugar-paste roping to the base of each tier.
8. If you want, use a #4 round tip to pipe small royal icing pearls along the top rim of each tier.

Crowning Moments
1. Gild the sugar-paste roping, any desired tiles, and the piping with gold dust.
2. Attach a chalice topper.
3. Adhere the pastillage Ursuline, winding it around the cake.

It was the Nika rebellion of 532. Empress Theodora leaned

over the balustrade and fixed her eyes on the horizon. In the

distance, she acknowledged the Barbarian troops approaching

Constantinople. Refusing to give up her throne—and reduce

her status to that of a fugitive—she declared: "Purple makes the

best winding robe." She would stay in Constantinople—where,

if she were executed, she could be buried in her chlamys.

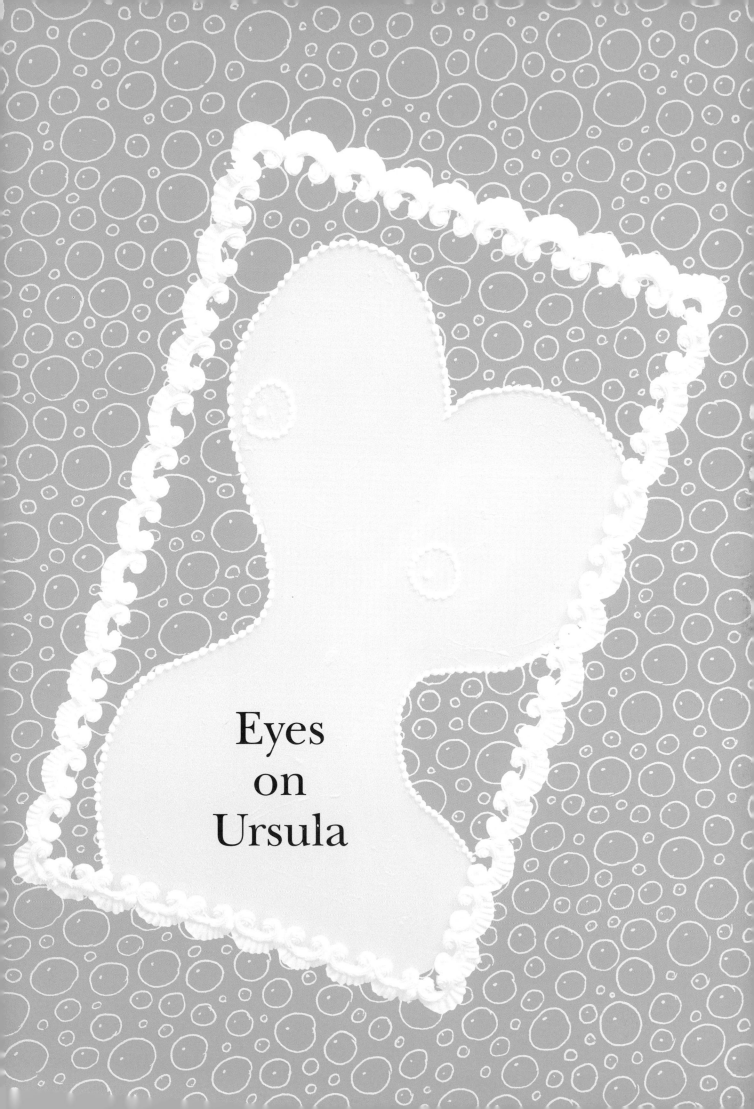

Eyes
on
Ursula

CAKE SIZES:
14-inch beveled tier; 10-inch and 8-inch round tiers; all 4 inches high

TOOLS AND INGREDIENTS:
Marzipan; pastry bag; #6 round tip; royal icing; green and blue food coloring; paintbrushes; sugar paste; pastillage; paper cornetta; gold dust and pearl dust finishes

MOTIFS AND TECHNIQUES:
Swags; painting with food coloring; royal icing pearls; atomic starbursts; polka dots; royal icing flourishes; sugar-paste roping; pastillage Ursuline; sugar paste tassels; sugar chalice topper; finishing with gold and pearl dust

DIRECTIONS:

1. Cover the cakes with marzipan.

First Tier

1. Attach the #6 round tip to a pastry bag filled with royal icing, and pipe royal icing swags around the tier.
2. Paint green below the swags and blue above the swags.
3. Pipe a royal icing pearl border along the base.
4. Apply atomic starbursts and a few polka dots below the swags.
5. Using the cornetta, pipe royal icing flourishes above the swags.
6. Adhere loops of sugar-paste roping between the bevels.

Second Tier

1. Using the cornetta, pipe royal icing flourishes around the tier.
2. Paint blue below the royal icing and green above.
3. Apply a gorgeous pastillage Ursuline smack in the middle of the tier.
4. Apply a few polka dots to the tier if you like.

Third Tier

1. Repeat method used for first tier.
2. Place sugar paste roping finished with sugar paste tassels along the top ledge of the tiers.

Crowning Moment

1. Apply a sugar chalice topper.
2. Finish the topper with gold and pearl dust as pictured.

This cake is many things. It's a shrine to Saint Ursula or a

memorial to Hester Prynne. It's a pedestal for a sugar chalice and a

showcase for sugar tassels. It's old, it's new; it's green, it's blue.

Other than blueberries, there is no blue food. But blue is a beautiful

color, especially when partnered with the right green. This

cake is an exercise in making choices of color, scale, and decoration.

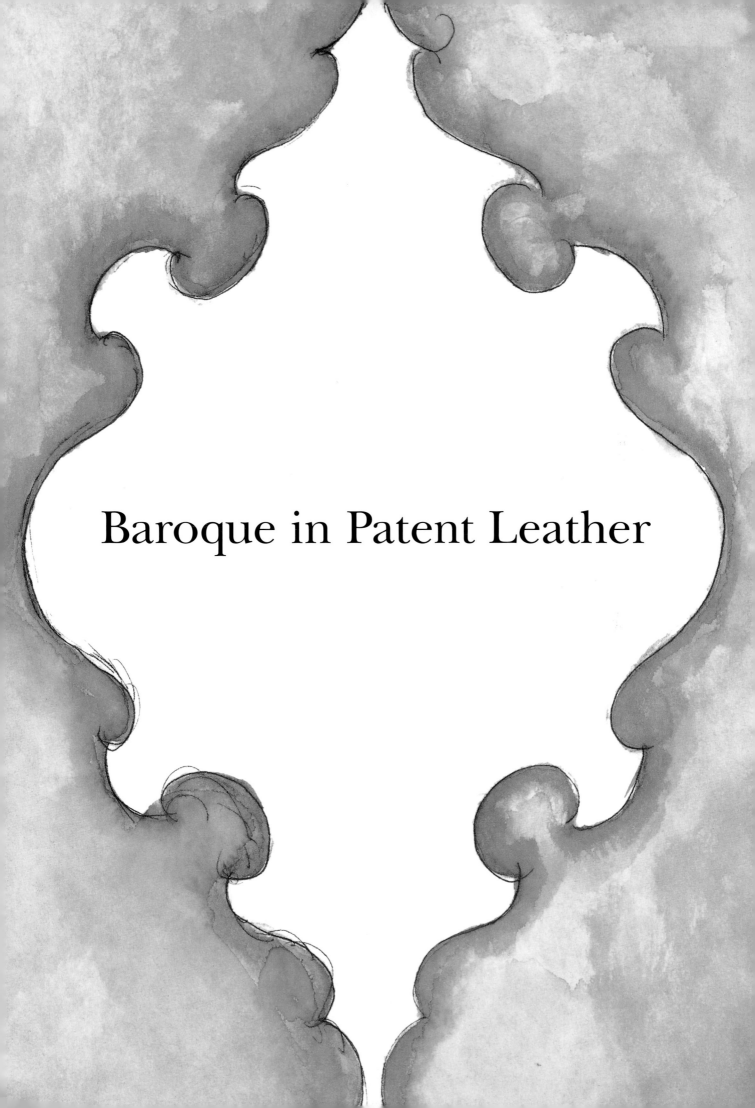

Baroque in Patent Leather

This cake was originally
inspired by a pair of
shoes I was lusting
after. They were pink
and orange patent-leather
platforms with an oversized pearly white eyelet tongue.
I wanted to make a patent-leather cake. Following
one of my late-night chats with the corn goddess,
I began mixing the colors: orange with a touch of
brown and black; and pink with a touch of black, making
it more like magenta. I was after the shiny plastic finish of patent
leather, so I mixed in lots of pearl dust. I got lost in a pink and orange
daydream, and that was the end of the shoe fetish.

I put the colors aside and let my mind wander. Instead of shoes and fashion
accessories, I was now looking for a way to combine these electric
colors into an old-world decorative setting. I wanted to use
the asymmetrical flourishes of a rococo picture frame.
But I wanted the contour of the cake itself to
complement those sugar-work decorations, so I decided
to carve swirls and curves into
the cake before
covering it with the
sugar paste. (See "How
to Sculpt the Tiers
of a Cake," page 90).

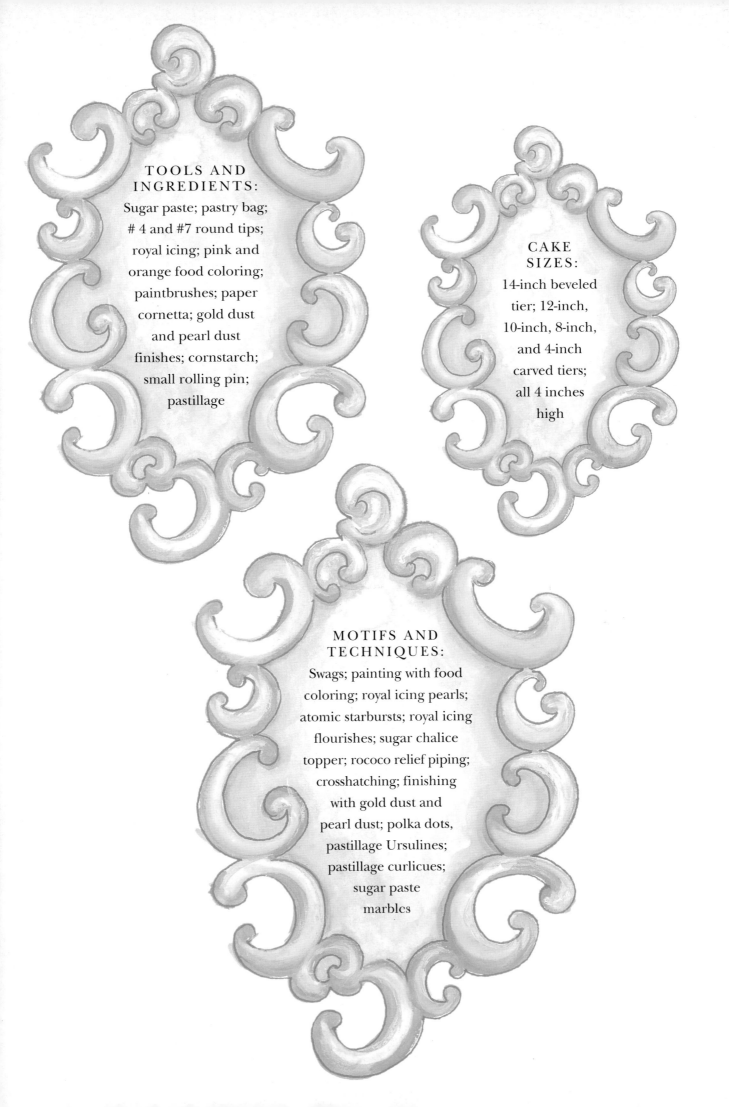

TOOLS AND INGREDIENTS:
Sugar paste; pastry bag; # 4 and #7 round tips; royal icing; pink and orange food coloring; paintbrushes; paper cornetta; gold dust and pearl dust finishes; cornstarch; small rolling pin; pastillage

CAKE SIZES:
14-inch beveled tier; 12-inch, 10-inch, 8-inch, and 4-inch carved tiers; all 4 inches high

MOTIFS AND TECHNIQUES:
Swags; painting with food coloring; royal icing pearls; atomic starbursts; royal icing flourishes; sugar chalice topper; rococo relief piping; crosshatching; finishing with gold dust and pearl dust; polka dots, pastillage Ursulines; pastillage curlicues; sugar paste marbles

DIRECTIONS:

1. Cover the cakes with sugar paste and dust a smooth, clean work surface with cornstarch.

First Tier

1. Attach the #7 round tip to a pastry bag filled with royal icing. Pipe swags around the tier.
2. Paint pink below the swags and orange above.
3. Pipe royal icing pearls around the bottom edge.
4. Apply atomic starburst motifs below the swags.
5. Using the cornetta, pipe royal icing flourishes above the swags.
6. Attach pastillage Ursulines between the bevels.

Second Tier

1. Paint the sides of the tier pink.
2. Paint the top ledge of the cake orange.
3. Pipe a royal icing pearl border along the bottom edge.
4. Attach the #7 round tip to the pastry bag and pipe rococo relief around the tiers.
5. When the icing is dry, use the #4 attachment to pipe miniature pearls along the rococo relief.
6. Adhere a few polka dots along the top ledge of the tier.

Third Tier

1. Pipe swags around the tier.
2. Paint pink below the swags and orange above.
3. Apply sugar-paste crosshatching beneath the swags. (You can also pipe on a crosshatching pattern with the straight edge of a #47 basket-weave tip.)
4. Pipe a pearl border along the bottom of the tier.

5. Apply atomic starbursts to some of the crosshatched intersections as desired.
6. Using a cornetta, pipe royal icing flourishes above the swags.

Fourth Tier

1. Repeat steps used for second tier.

Fifth Tier

1. Paint the entire tier orange.
2. Apply sugar-paste (or royal icing) crosshatching.
3. Pipe a royal icing pearl border along the bottom of the tier.
4. Apply atomic starbursts to crosshatched intersections as desired.

Crowning Moments

1. Apply a sugar chalice topper, or pastillage curlicues and sugar-paste marbles.
2. Gild the swags, crosshatching, and desired areas of atomic starbursts with gold dust.
3. Finish the pearls, drapery, filigrees, and pastillage curlicues, along with desired areas of the starbursts, with pearl dust.

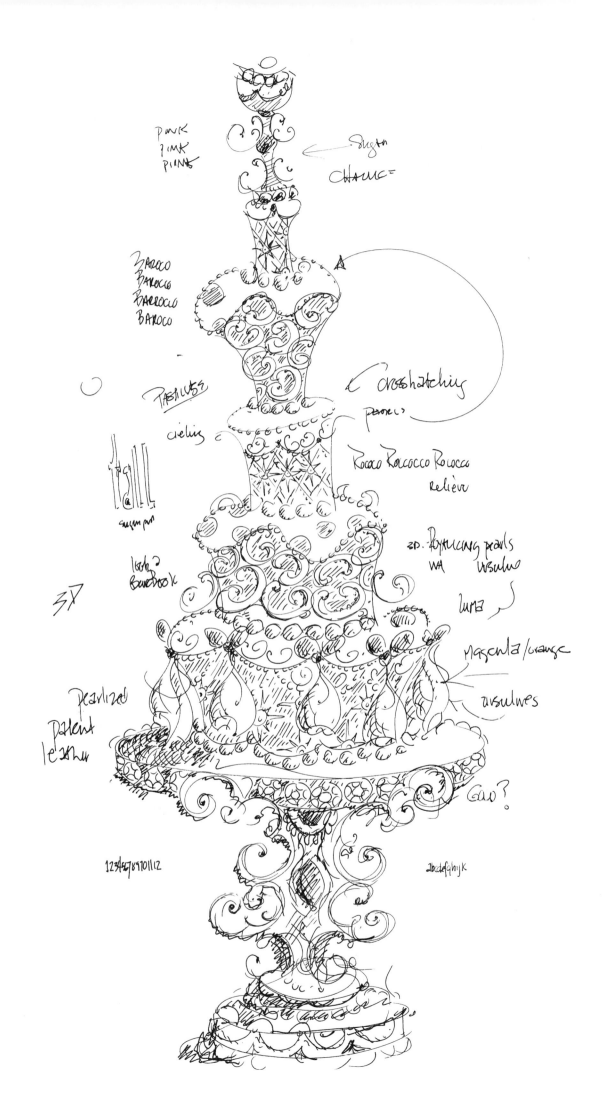

PINK
PINK
PINK

Sugar
CHALICE

BAROCO
BAROCO
BAROCCO
BAROCO

PASTILLES

cieling

Crosshatching
pearls

Rococo Rococco Rococco
relieve

3D. Roxouching pearls
wa ursulve

luma

Magenta/orange

ursulves

16th
Benedbook

3D

Pearlized
Patent
leather

Gau?

1234567891011112   abcdefghijk

I got lost

in a pink and

orange

daydream.

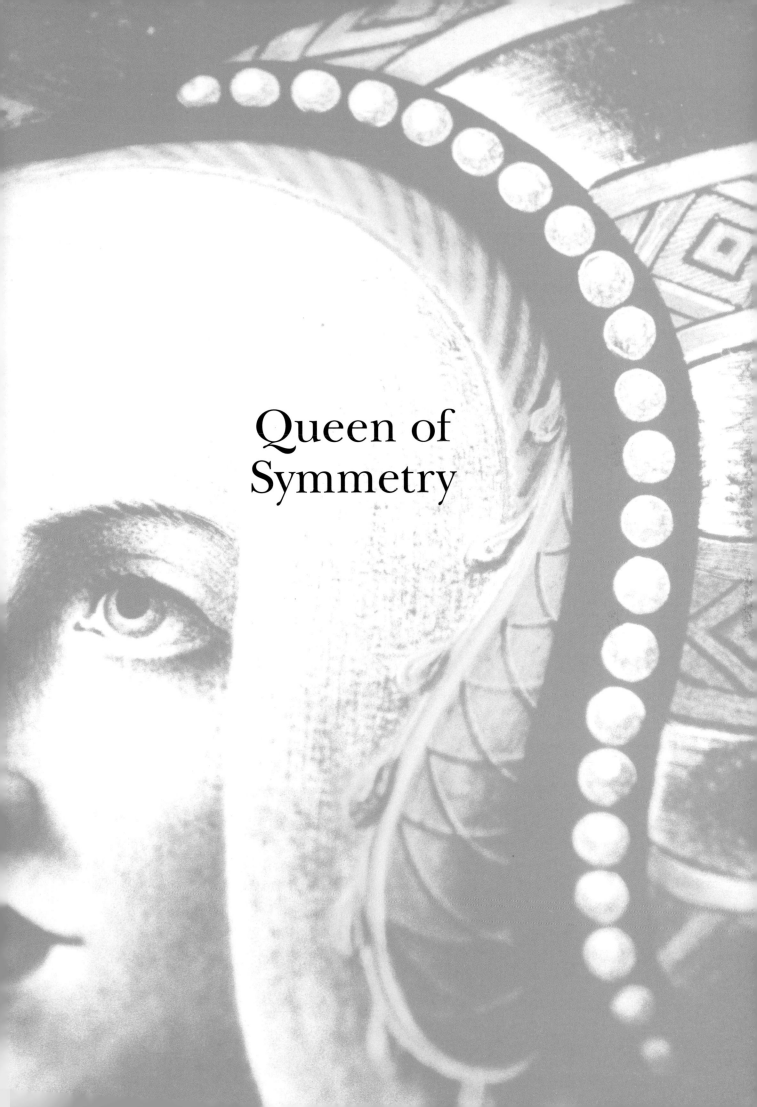

Queen of
Symmetry

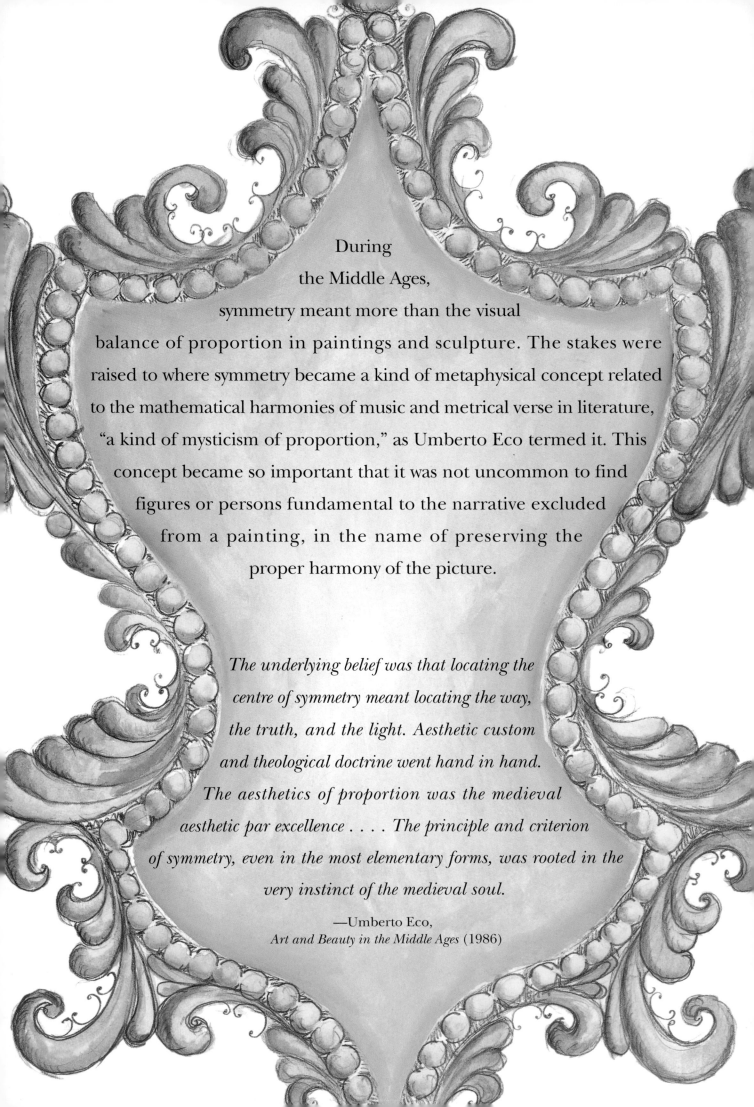

During
the Middle Ages,
symmetry meant more than the visual
balance of proportion in paintings and sculpture. The stakes were
raised to where symmetry became a kind of metaphysical concept related
to the mathematical harmonies of music and metrical verse in literature,
"a kind of mysticism of proportion," as Umberto Eco termed it. This
concept became so important that it was not uncommon to find
figures or persons fundamental to the narrative excluded
from a painting, in the name of preserving the
proper harmony of the picture.

The underlying belief was that locating the
centre of symmetry meant locating the way,
the truth, and the light. Aesthetic custom
and theological doctrine went hand in hand.
The aesthetics of proportion was the medieval
aesthetic par excellence . . . . The principle and criterion
of symmetry, even in the most elementary forms, was rooted in the
very instinct of the medieval soul.

—Umberto Eco,
Art and Beauty in the Middle Ages (1986)

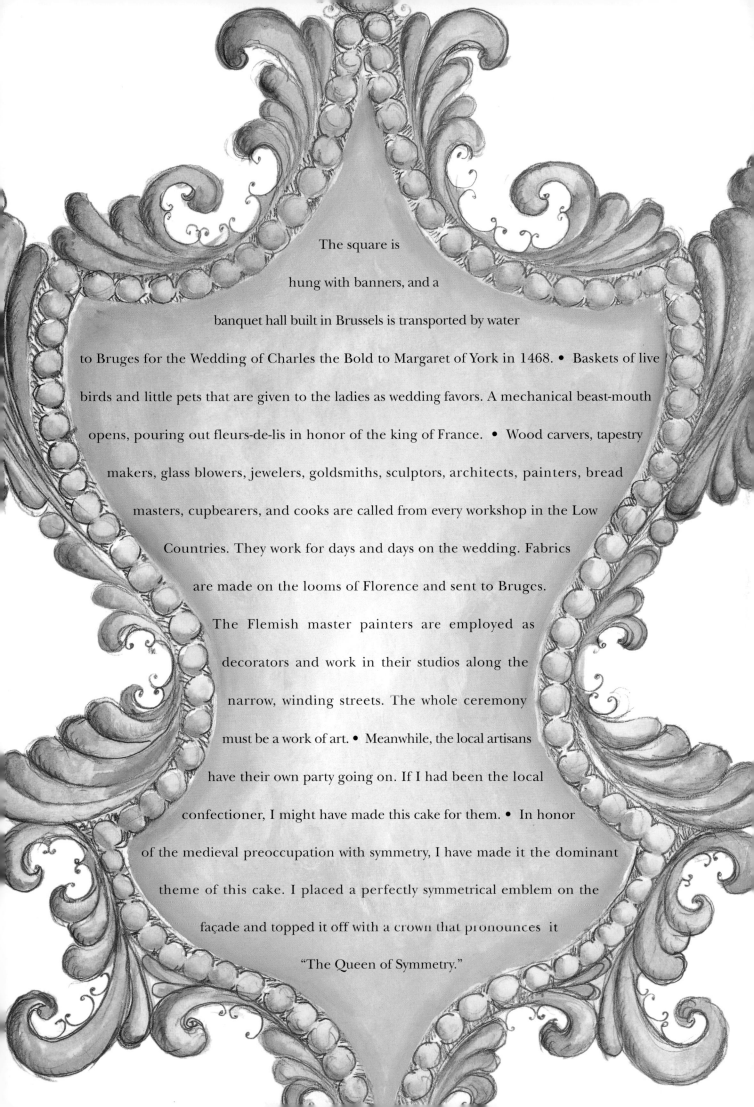

The square is

hung with banners, and a

banquet hall built in Brussels is transported by water

to Bruges for the Wedding of Charles the Bold to Margaret of York in 1468. • Baskets of live

birds and little pets that are given to the ladies as wedding favors. A mechanical beast-mouth

opens, pouring out fleurs-de-lis in honor of the king of France. • Wood carvers, tapestry

makers, glass blowers, jewelers, goldsmiths, sculptors, architects, painters, bread

masters, cupbearers, and cooks are called from every workshop in the Low

Countries. They work for days and days on the wedding. Fabrics

are made on the looms of Florence and sent to Bruges.

The Flemish master painters are employed as

decorators and work in their studios along the

narrow, winding streets. The whole ceremony

must be a work of art. • Meanwhile, the local artisans

have their own party going on. If I had been the local

confectioner, I might have made this cake for them. • In honor

of the medieval preoccupation with symmetry, I have made it the dominant

theme of this cake. I placed a perfectly symmetrical emblem on the

façade and topped it off with a crown that pronounces it

"The Queen of Symmetry."

DIRECTIONS:

1. Cover the cakes with the violet marzipan.
2. Adhere sugar-paste roping around the bottom edge of all tiers.
3. Attach the #4 round tip to a pastry bag filled with royal icing. Pipe swags around the first, third, fifth, and seventh tiers.
4. Pipe a delicate rococo relief design around the second, fourth, sixth, and eight tiers.
5. Embellish the swags and rococo relief with royal icing pearls.
6. Adhere polka dots along the top edge of the first seven tiers.

"Queen of Symmetry" Emblems

1. Start constructing the emblem from the bottom by leaning two curlicues of equal size against the bottom tier. When they're symmetrically positioned, adhere them to the cake façade with royal icing at the point of contact. Let it dry in place.
2. Using an oval cutter or freehand, cut an oval medallion from a sheet of pastillage. When it's dry, gently rest an oval medallion directly in the center of the opposing curlicues. Adhere the medallion to the cake façade with royal icing at the point of contact. Let it dry in place.
3. Repeat this process all the way to the top tier, or until you are satisfied with its design.
4. Apply sugar-paste crosshatching to the medallions.
5. Frame the medallions with royal icing pearls, and embellish the curlicues with royal icing pearls.

Crowning Moments

1. Gild all roping, swags, curlicues, and crosshatching with gold dust.
2. Finish all pearls with pearl dust.
3. Adhere the crown to the top of the cake with royal icing.

CAKE SIZES:
10-inch, 9-inch, 8-inch, 7-inch, 6-inch, 5-inch, 4-inch, and 3-inch tiers; all 2 inches high

MOTIFS AND TECHNIQUES:
Sugar-paste roping; swags; rococo relief; royal icing pearls; polka dots; pastillage curlicues (nine opposing sets); crosshatching; finishing with gold dust and pearl dust; crown for "Medieval Bruges"

TOOLS AND INGREDIENTS:
Violet marzipan; small amount of mint-green marzipan; sugar paste; pastry bag; #4 round tip; royal icing; pastillage; oval cutter (optional); gold dust and pearl dust finishes

Cakewalk through Barcelona

This morning, the merciless clamor of shop gates opening beneath my window woke me up. This is a familiar sound, which I associate with early mornings and work in bakeries. It took me a moment to realize where I was. Years ago, while working in a Greenwich Village bakery, I lived above a Czech hatmaker. I didn't need an alarm clock because he too was an early riser. So at 6 A.M., six days a week, those rumbling gates would catapult me from my futon right into the shower. This morning, however, I lay in bed musing over the details of last night's typically late Catalan dinner after hearing those metal gates. I stumble to the window of my hotel room, open the shutters, and look out onto Barcelona's Placeta del Pi (Square of the Pine Tree). This fine little square is flanked by a handful of cafés, bars, a hair salon, a pharmacy, a cutlery shop, a wine store, and my modest hotel. In the center of the square sits a church—La Esglesia de Santa Maria del Pi (built between 1322 and 1486), an austere early Gothic structure, sporting a massive Spanish Romanesque portal and a spectacular rose window. It stands on the site of a pre-Christian Paleolithic building, and is named for a very special pine tree that once grew in its place. Although it isn't a huge or particularly ornate church by Gothic standards, its smoky stone mass gives an almost sober tone to this charming little square.

The shops are opening. One man in a woolen vest and cap sweeps the radius of his piece of the *placeta*. Above him, a fiftyish woman in a turquoise and pink floral house-dress leans over her terrace, ringing excess water from her laundry. I am sure she is going to drop water on the man. Across the way the lights are on over a kitchen table. There is movement inside—children, I'm guessing, getting ready for school. Now the man in the vest holds a stick and he's poking bits of trash and leaves from the cracks in the cobblestones.

A humorously small truck suddenly zips into the plaza and stops short beneath my window. The driver hops out, makes his delivery, jumps back into the van, and disappears into a side street. He's the pastry man, and my cue. I go down to get one of those pastries while they're hot. Along with my third *café con leche*, I ask for my pastry, which comes sliding across the marble bar resting on a cocktail napkin and stops amiably right in front of me. It's a triangle—warm and flaky, dusted with confectioners' sugar. Anticipating an apricot preserve or pastry cream filling, I detect the beany texture of quince paste (*membrillo*) and cinnamon. I am immediately reminded of Barcelona's brief yet still resonant link with North Africa.

Making my way outside, I ask a waiter setting up tables at a neighboring café, "Which way to Le Seu?" (the Barcelona cathedral). His sweeping gestures suggest that there are many ways to Le Seu, and that it's up to me to decide which route to take. I choose Carrer de Girona, one of the larger arteries leading out of the *placeta*. The street is already bustling with people on their way to work. They brush along stone façades to let others pass. These stones are old, like velvet to the touch. And I discover a treasure behind the velvet stones— Forn de Pasde Artesa, a lovely little shop that carries convent sweets, which are cakes and pastries baked by Spanish nuns. Now the cake-walk begins.

I make my way out of the Gothic quarter, pass through the Placa de Catalunya, and continue north on the Passeig de Gracia, where I encounter a feast of modernist architecture, especially the work of Antoni Gaudí. I thought, now here is a cake decorator who burst out of the kitchen and went on to make cakes to live in, have cocktail parties in, and (in the case of the Sagrada Familia, a church he left unfinished at his death) worship in.

CAKE SIZES:
12-inch beveled
tier; 10-inch,
6-inch sculpted
tiers; 8-inch
round tier; all 4
inches high

MOTIFS AND
TECHNIQUES:
Sugar-paste roping;
pastillage Ursulines;
polka dots; sugar mosaic;
royal icing pearls; painting
with food coloring; swags;
crosshatching; atomic
starbursts; chalice
topper; finishing
with gold dust and
pearl dust

TOOLS AND
INGREDIENTS:
Light blue marzipan;
orange marzipan;
sugar paste; royal icing;
pastillage; paper
cornetta; yellow
and blue royal icing;
gold dust and pearl
dust finishes

DIRECTIONS:
1. Cover the second and fourth tiers with marzipan and the first and third tiers with blue marzipan.

First Tier
1. Adhere sugar-paste roping around the bottom of the tier.
2. Attach pastillage Ursulines between the bevels.
3. Adhere orange polka dots thoughtfully onto the blue marzipan surface.
4. Pipe royal icing fleurs-de-lis between the polka dots.

Second Tier
1. Apply a white-tiled mosaic pattern to the tier with yellow royal icing mortar. Paint tiles as desired.
2. Pipe a pearl border along the top ledge and around selected mosaic patterns.
3. Apply sugar-paste roping around the bottom of the tier.

Third Tier
1. Pipe a swag border around the top of the tier.
2. Apply royal icing crosshatching beneath the swags.
3. Gently drape sugar-paste roping across the gathers in the royal icing swags.
4. Apply atomic starbursts to selected intersections of the crosshatching.

Fourth Tier
1. Apply a white-tiled mosaic pattern to the tier with blue royal icing mortar.
2. Pipe pearl borders around selected mosaic tiles.
3. Pipe a pearl border along the top edge of the tier.
4. Roll out a sheet of pastillage, cut out four oval medallions, and apply them beneath the curves in the tier with a dab of royal icing. Paint the ovals as desired.
5. Pipe a string of small pearls around the ovals.
6. Adhere sugar-paste roping around the bottom edge of the tier.

Crowning Moments
1. Adhere a sugar chalice topper to the top of the cake.
2. Gild the sugar-paste roping, crosshatching, pastillage Ursulines, swags, and selected areas of the atomic starbursts with gold dust.
3. Finish the pearl borders, fleur-de-lis piping, and selected areas of the starbursts with pearl dust.

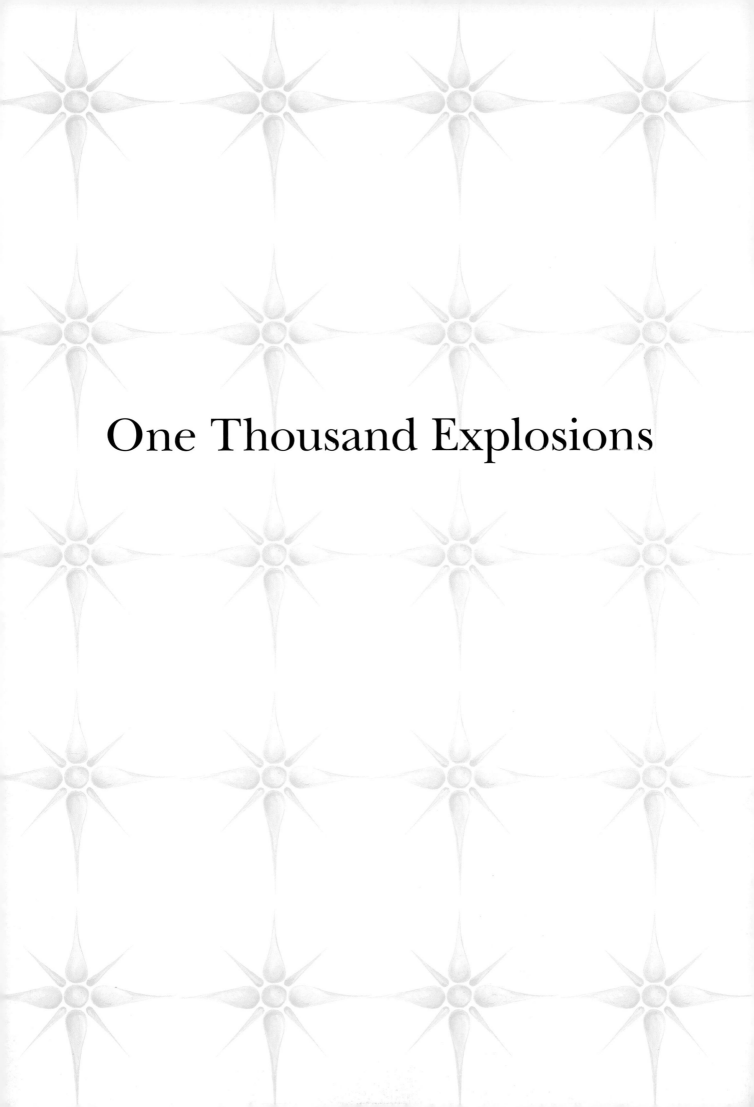

One Thousand Explosions

Sometimes, the story of the object is secondary to the way the object looks. I had no story in mind while making this cake, but I did wish to make an old-fashioned space-age cake with a touch of household imagery. This was achieved by combining those sobering royal icing swags with space-age atomic starbursts and retro-pop flowers.

CAKE SIZES:
18-inch beveled tier;
12-inch, 10-inch, 8-inch,
and 6-inch round tiers;
all 4 inches high

MOTIFS AND TECHNIQUES:
Swags; painting with
food coloring; decal recall flowers; royal icing
pearls; flourishes; atomic starbursts; polka dots;
sugar-paste roping; sugar-paste tassels; finishing
with gold dust and pearl dust;
sugar chalice topper

TOOLS AND INGREDIENTS:
Sugar paste; pastry bag;
#5 round tip; royal icing; light blue, lime green, and
magenta food coloring; paintbrush; gold dust, and pearl
dust finishes; paper cornetta

DIRECTIONS:
1. Cover the cakes with sugar paste.

First Tier
1. Attach the #5 round tip to a pastry bag filled with royal icing. Pipe swags around the top of the tier.
2. Paint flowers beneath the swags.
3. Pipe a royal icing pearl border around the bottom edge.
4. Fill the cornetta with royal icing and pipe flourishes above the swags.
5. Using the cornetta filled with royal icing, pipe fleurs-de-lis between the flowers.
6. Pipe pearls around the flower petals.

Second Tier
1. Pipe swags around the top of the tier.
2. Paint lime green beneath the swags and light blue above.
3. Pipe a pearl border around the bottom edge.
4. Apply atomic starbursts and polka dots below the swags.

Third Tier
1. Use same method as first tier, except invert the color scheme of the flowers.

Fourth Tier
1. Use same method as second tier, except the invert the color scheme above and below the swags.

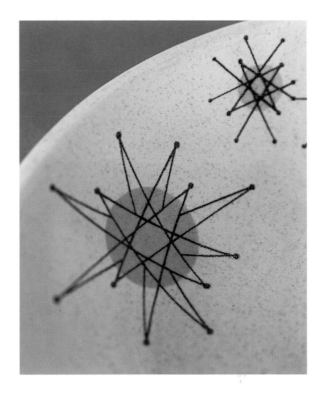

Fifth Tier
1. Repeat the flower pattern from the first tier but omit the swag barrier.
2. Pipe pearls around the flower petals.
3. Echo the royal icing swags with sugar-paste roping.

Crowning Moments
1. Drape a few sugar-paste ropes along the ledge of the second tier and attach sugar-paste tassels to the ends.
2. Gild the pearls around the flower petals, the swags, and the filigree piping of the first tier with gold dust. Do the same with the sugar-paste roping, tassels, and selected areas of the starbursts elsewhere on the cake.
3. Finish the pearl borders, fleurs-de-lis, polka dots, selected areas of the starbursts, and the filigree piping on the third tier with pearl dust.
4. Adhere loops of sugar-paste roping with royal icing from the gathers of selected swags on the second and fourth tiers.
5. Adhere a sugar chalice topper to the top.

THE RECIPES

Basic Recipes

MARZIPAN

Take...blanched almonds . . . white sugar . . . Rosewater . . . and Damask water . . . Beate the Almondes with a little of the same water, and grind them till they be small: set them on a few coales of fyre, till they waxe thicke, them beat them again with the sugar, fine . . . mixe the sweet waters and them together, and . . .fashion your Marchpane . . .and ye maye while it is moysse stiche it full of . . . sundrie colours. If it be thorough dryed . . . a Marchpane will last mant yeares.

—*Partridge's classic 16th-century cookbook* (1584)

Like bread, wine, olive oil, and honey, marzipan is an ancient food with an air of significance. It was introduced in Europe, by way of the Middle East, toward the end of the twelfth century. A sweet, intensely almondy, malleable paste, it is rolled out like sugar paste and draped over cakes or shaped into fruits, figurines, and edible sculptures. The best marzipan is made with fresh almond paste, which starts with almond flour. This is made by blanching and peeling the almonds and running them through a "raffinatrice" (refiner)—like a huge pasta maker, with massive marble rollers that grind the almonds into flour—before adding sugar. (Marble is non-porous and always a little cooler than room temperature, which helps prevent nut oils from heating up and liquefying.) A raffinatrice is hard to find, so the next best way to make fresh marzipan is the real old-fashioned way: by first grinding almonds with a mortar and pestle. The following is a much easier method. (It can also be purchased premade; see "Sources and Merchants," page 218.)

Makes: Enough to cover one 10-inch-diameter by 4-inch-high cake
Tools: Standing electric mixer with paddle attachment; rubber spatula

INGREDIENTS:
8 ounces (1/2 pound) almond paste
3 cups confectioners' sugar
1 teaspoon rose-blossom water, orange-blossom water, or pure vanilla extract
5 tablespoons light corn syrup (or glucose)

DIRECTIONS:
1. Break the almond paste into pieces and place in the bowl of a standing electric mixer. Begin mixing at low speed with a paddle attachment.
2. Add half the confectioners' sugar, and all the rose water and corn syrup. Mix at low speed until well incorporated.
3. Scrape down the sides of the bowl with a rubber spatula and add the remaining confectioners' sugar.
4. Transfer the marzipan to a smooth work surface and knead until smooth, adding small amounts of confectioners' sugar if the dough is too sticky. Don't add too much sugar or the marzipan may dry out and crack.
5. Shape the marzipan into a smooth round ball and double-wrap in plastic wrap. Place in an airtight container. Marzipan will keep for up to four months in the refrigerator in an airtight container.

SUGAR PASTE
(ROLLED FONDANT)

Sugar paste is a soft, malleable, sweet, doughlike mixture that is rolled out in sheets, then draped over and fitted around the cake tiers. It has a smooth, matte finish reminiscent of porcelain. It can also be used to make those sugar fruits and figurines that make such lovely decorations. If you're short on time, you can buy premade sugar paste or rolled fondant at a cake-decorating supplier. The prefab sugar paste is easier to work with—and some might even say it tastes better.

Makes: Enough to cover a 10-inch-diameter by 4-inch-high cake

Tools: Flour sifter; standing electric mixer with paddle attachment; double boiler; rubber spatula; metal bench scraper to maintain a smooth work surface

NOTE: *Sugar paste should not be refrigerated because it will become very sticky.*

INGREDIENTS:

2 pounds confectioners' sugar

1 tablespoon unflavored gelatin

3 tablespoons cold water

$1/2$ cup light corn syrup (or glucose)

$1^{1}/2$ tablespoons glycerin (see "Sources and Merchants," page 218)

1 tablespoon pure vanilla extract

DIRECTIONS:

1. Sift $1^{1}/2$ pounds of the confectioners' sugar into a large standing mixer bowl. Set aside.
2. In the top of a double boiler, stir the gelatin into the cold water. Dissolve over simmering water until clear, Remove from the heat and stir in the corn syrup, glycerin, and vanilla.
3. With the standing mixer turning on low speed, slowly pour the gelatin mixture into the reserved sugar. Scrape down the sides with a rubber spatula. Continue beating on medium speed until well combined and very sticky.
4. Scrape the sticky fondant onto a clean work surface and knead in the remaining $1/2$ pound confectioners' sugar, a little at a time. Knead until a pliable dough forms.
5. Shape the fondant into a smooth ball. Cover with plastic wrap and place in airtight container overnight. Do not refrigerate.

PASTILLAGE

Like sugar paste, pastillage is a sugar-based mixture that is rolled out like a pie dough. It can be molded or shaped into cups, bowls, plaques, bows, and paisley shapes. It contains gum tracaganth, which serves as a "catalyst" between the confectioners' sugar and the water, causing the paste to harden very much like porcelain. It's great to work with, but it dries very quickly, so you must work fast. You can purchase premade gum paste (pastillage that contains softening agents such as glycerin or glucose, which makes it easier to work with) at a cake-decorating supplier. Free-form pastillage motifs such as paisleys, curlicues, bows, and faux daisies can be stored in an airtight container in a cool, dry place.

Makes: Approximately 2 cups
Tools: Flour sifter; standing electric mixer with nonreactive mixing bowl and paddle attachment; plastic spatula; metal bench scraper to maintain a smooth work surface

INGREDIENTS:
2 pounds confectioners' sugar, sifted
3 tablespoons gum tracaganth
    (see "Sources and Merchants," page 218)
1/2 cup water
Cornstarch, for dusting

DIRECTIONS:
1. Sift the sugar and the gum tracaganth into the bowl of a standing electric mixer.
2. Add the water and mix thoroughly, scraping down the sides occasionally with a rubber spatula.
3. Transfer the pastillage to a smooth surface dusted with cornstarch.
4. Knead until the mixture forms a smooth, pliable mass. Wrap in plastic wrap and store in an airtight container overnight. Do not refrigerate.

ROYAL ICING

A meringue-like icing that dries very hard, royal icing is used with a pastry bag or paper cornetta for piping intricate designs and relief work on a cake.

Makes: 2 1/2 cups
Tools: Standing electric mixer with paddle attachment, rubber spatula

INGREDIENTS:
2 large egg whites at room temperature
1 pound confectioners' sugar
Juice of 1/2 lemon

DIRECTIONS:
1. Place the egg whites in the bowl of a standing electric mixer and beat on medium speed until loosened (about 30 seconds).
2. Gradually add the confectioners' sugar, 1 cup at a time, beating continuously.
3. Add the lemon juice. Scrape down the sides of the bowl with a rubber spatula. Continue beating until the icing holds its shape (4–5 minutes).
4. Cover the bowl with a damp cloth to keep the icing from drying out. After you've iced your cake, refrigerate any remaining icing in an airtight container for up to one week.

Personal Favorites

CANDIED ORANGES

Within days of my return from Barcelona, I was laboring over a hot stove trying to reproduce the succulent candied oranges that had sustained me throughout my cakewalk. I loved them so much that I painted oranges on the bottom tier of my Cakewalk through Barcelona (page 182). These are delicious by themselves, but I also like to chop them up and add them to cake fillings. They can be stored in an airtight container for up to one month.

Makes: 32 pieces

Tools: Large saucepan; slotted spoon; baking sheet; parchment paper; baking rack; paper bag

INGREDIENTS:

8 medium navel oranges, preferably organic, quartered lengthwise

Water

5$\frac{1}{2}$ cups sugar

$\frac{1}{4}$ cup light corn syrup

DIRECTIONS:

1. In a large saucepan, cover the oranges with water and bring to a boil. Reduce the heat and simmer for 30 minutes. Using a slotted spoon, transfer the oranges to a baking sheet lined with parchment. Discard the water.

2. In the same saucepan, combine 4 cups of the sugar with the corn syrup and 2 cups of water and bring to a boil over moderately high heat; stir constantly until the sugar is dissolved. Add the oranges and cook over low heat, stirring occasionally until they begin to look glassy (about 1$\frac{1}{2}$ hours).

3. Raise the heat to high and boil vigorously for 7 minutes; the orange rinds will begin to look translucent. Remove from heat and let the oranges cool in the syrup. Using a slotted spoon, transfer the oranges to a baking sheet lined with parchment paper. Reserve the cooking syrup. Let the oranges stand uncovered overnight, or until they are sticky to the touch.

4. Bring the reserved syrup to a boil over high heat. Add the oranges and boil for 10 minutes. Let cool completely in the syrup. Using a slotted spoon, transfer the oranges skin side down to a baking rack. Let stand until they are sticky.

5. Put the remaining 1$\frac{1}{2}$ cups of sugar in a paper bag. Add the oranges and shake until well coated. Transfer the oranges to a baking sheet lined with parchment and let dry; sugar them again if they still seem moist. Let the oranges stand uncovered overnight, or for several days.

FLOURLESS CHOCOLATE YULE LOG

This is the first cake I ever made, and it is very dear to my heart. I have eaten it at Christmas every year of my life. It bakes into a thin, slightly spongy, chocolatey sheet cake that is filled with unsweetened whipped cream, that is rolled into a log shape, and sprinkled with unsweetened cocoa. The taste of each component—the whipped cream, the semisweet chocolate mixed with coffee, the cocoa, down to the subtle flavor of the baked egg white—gives it a sort of bittersweet, dairy-cream, simplicity. It is wonderful.

Makes: 8–10 servings

Tools: 12-inch by 18-inch baking sheet; parchment paper; double boiler; 2 large mixing bowls; electric hand mixer with whisk attachment; rubber spatula; large metal spatula

INGREDIENTS:

6 ounces semisweet chocolate, chopped
5 large eggs, separated
2/3 cup sugar
3 tablespoons espresso coffee (warm, not hot)
1 1/2 cups heavy cream
Unsweetened cocoa powder, for dusting

DIRECTIONS:

Preparation

1. Preheat the oven to 325 degrees. Line the baking sheet with parchment paper.
2. Melt the chocolate in a double boiler over gently simmering water.
3. In a large mixing bowl, whisk the egg yolks with the sugar until thick and lemon-colored. While whisking, add the melted chocolate in a slow stream, followed by the espresso.
4. In a large bowl, beat the egg whites until stiff.
5. With a rubber spatula, gently fold the egg whites into the chocolate mixture until incorporated; don't overmix.
6. Pour the batter evenly onto the prepared baking sheet and bake for about 15 minutes or until a toothpick comes out clean; don't overbake. Remove the cake from the oven; while still on the baking sheet, cover with a slightly damp towel. Let cool for 1 hour.
7. Whisk the cream until soft peaks form. Set aside in the refrigerator.

Assembly

1. Place a sheet of parchment at least 3 inches longer than the cake on the work surface. Remove the towel from the cake and sprinkle with cocoa. Loosen the cake's edges from the baking sheet, and quickly invert the cake onto the parchment.
2. Spread the whipped cream onto the cake.
3. Starting with the long ends nearest you, grasp each corner of the parchment paper and lift it up, then turn the cake over itself to roll up like a jelly roll. Using a large metal spatula, transfer to a platter. Sprinkle with cocoa and serve.

SUNDAY PANCAKE

Derived from an old Craig Claiborne recipe in the *New York Times,* this is one of the most delicious breakfast pastries in the entire world. It's the perfect combination of light, heavy, sweet, and eggy. It is a pleasure to make because along with its excellent flavor, it looks like a miniature mountain range complete with valleys of browned butter and lemon juice. This is also great served with fresh peaches, berries, or any fruit you prefer.

Makes: 4–6 servings

Tools: Mixing bowl; whisk;
    12-inch oven-proof skillet

INGREDIENTS:

$1/2$ cup milk

2 large eggs, lightly beaten

$1/2$ cup all-purpose flour

6 tablespoons unsalted butter

Confectioners' sugar

Lemon juice

DIRECTIONS:

1. Preheat the oven to 425 degrees.
2. In a mixing bowl, combine the milk, eggs, and flour. Beat lightly, leaving the batter a little lumpy.
3. Melt the butter in a 12-inch skillet. When very hot, pour in the batter. Bake in the preheated oven until set and golden brown (15 to 20 minutes).
4. Sprinkle with confectioners' sugar and return to the oven for 1 more minute.
5. Remove from the oven. Sprinkle with more confectioners' sugar, squeeze lemon juice on top, and serve.

CHERRY CRESCENTS
FROM CRESCENT STREET

These cookies are derived from the vanilla-nut crescent recipe my grandmother baked from *The Settlement Cookbook*. I have added pistachio nuts and dried cherries to Grandma Helen's original recipe.

Makes: About 40 cookies

Tools: Food processor; mixing bowls; electric hand mixer; baking sheet; parchment paper

INGREDIENTS:

$1/2$ cup dried cherries, reconstituted in 1 cup hot water

$1/2$ cup unsalted, blanched pistachios

$1/2$ cup unsalted, blanched, skinned almonds

$3/4$ cup ($1 1/2$ sticks) unsalted butter

1 large egg yolk

1 teaspoon pure vanilla extract

$1 1/4$ cups sifted all-purpose flour

$1/2$ cup confectioners' sugar, plus $1/4$ cup for dusting

$1/8$ teaspoon salt

DIRECTIONS:

1. Drain the cherries and finely chop them.
2. Pulse the pistachios in a food processor until very fine and almost powdered. Transfer to a bowl. Repeat the process with the almonds.
3. Cream the butter with an electric mixer. Add the egg yolk and vanilla and mix until combined.
4. Add the chopped pistachios and almonds, the flour, the cherries, $1/2$ cup of the confectioners' sugar, and the salt, and mix until thoroughly incorporated.
5. Turn the dough out onto a well-floured board. The dough should be very sticky, so make sure your hands and the surface are well floured. Divide the dough in half and roll each half into $1 1/2$-inch round logs (see instructions for making sugar-paste roping, page 53). Cover the cookie dough with plastic wrap and refrigerate overnight.
6. Preheat the oven to 325 degrees.
7. Cut the chilled dough into $1/2$-inch-thick slices and shape into crescents. Arrange the crescents on a baking sheet lined with parchment.
8. Bake the crescents until set but not brown (about 25 minutes). Remove from the oven and allow to cool completely. Lightly dust the crescent cookies with the remaining $1/4$ cup of confectioners' sugar and serve.

Cakes for Decorating

Let the truth be known. The world suffers no shortage of excellent cake recipes. I have tasted endless configurations of butter, eggs, flour, and sugar. The following cake recipes are all great, but what makes them exceptional is how I fill them. To keep the cakes moist, I slice my layers thin, and top each layer with just the right amount of filling, so that every bite has the perfect ratio of cake to filling. I am also cautious with preserves. When used sparingly, preserves can add nice acidity or "color" to the cake's flavor. To avoid making a "jelly-filled cake," press a small amount of good-quality preserves into the cake layers. A cake should maintain its moisture and freshness from the moment you begin slicing the layers until the last bite is gone. If your cake is dry, you may be able to save it by lightly splashing each layer with a flavored simple syrup (see recipe, page 210).

The following recipes are my current favorites. They are all moist, delicious, and easy to work with.

In order to have the 4-inch-high façade needed to decorate most of my cakes, these recipes yield two 10-inch cakes. This usually leaves me with a few extra sliced layers. They can be frozen for two weeks, but wrap the cakes very thoroughly with plastic wrap, followed by a final wrap of tin foil.

CHOCOLATE BLACKOUT CAKE

This recipe was given to me by my friend Carrie, a pastry chef par excellence. She insisted it was the most delicious and versatile chocolate cake she had ever baked. She's right. The secret is buttermilk (which keeps the cake moist) and a little extra salt (which adds a wonderful sharpness to chocolate flavors). It's fudgy and very easy to make, a dream to work with, and delicious to eat.

Makes: Two 10-inch cakes, 12–15 servings

Tools: Two 10-inch round cake pans; 2 large mixing bowls; flour sifter; rubber spatula; cake tester; cooling rack

INGREDIENTS:

$2\frac{1}{3}$ cups all-purpose flour

$1\frac{1}{2}$ cups unsweetened cocoa powder

$1\frac{1}{4}$ teaspoons salt

1 tablespoon baking soda

1 tablespoon baking powder

3 cups sugar

5 large eggs

1 tablespoon pure vanilla extract

$1\frac{1}{2}$ cups buttermilk

$\frac{3}{4}$ cup ($1\frac{1}{2}$ sticks) unsalted butter, melted

$1\frac{1}{2}$ cups strong coffee (or 2 tablespoons instant espresso with $1\frac{1}{2}$ cups warm water)

DIRECTIONS:

1. Preheat the oven to 350 degrees. Butter and flour two 10-inch round cake pans.

2. Sift the flour, cocoa, salt, baking soda, and baking powder into a large mixing bowl. Stir in the sugar.

3. In another bowl, combine the eggs and vanilla extract, then mix them into the dry ingredients. Add the buttermilk, melted butter, and coffee. Scrape the batter into the prepared cake pans.

4. Bake the cakes until set around the edges and a cake tester inserted in the center comes out clean (about 50 minutes).

5. Let the cakes cool in their pans, then invert them onto a rack.

BUTTER CAKE

This is rich and buttery and similar to pound cake. Sour cream makes it a little tangy, while the top of the cake bakes crisp and sugary. I choose not to trim it off when layering the cake because it adds a crunchy sweetness to the cake layers. By simply adding lemon zest and lemon juice to the recipe, this cake is instantly transformed into a fabulous lemon butter cake.

Makes: Two 10-inch cakes, 12–15 servings

Tools: Two 10-inch round cake pans; flour sifter; 2 large mixing bowls; electric mixer; rubber spatula; cake tester; cooling rack

INGREDIENTS:

5 cups all-purpose flour

2 teaspoons baking powder

1 teaspoon baking soda

1 teaspoon salt

2 cups (4 sticks) unsalted butter, softened

$4\frac{1}{2}$ cups sugar, plus $\frac{1}{2}$ cup for sprinkling

6 large eggs

2 teaspoons pure vanilla extract

Finely grated zest of 4 lemons (for lemon cake)

Juice of 1 lemon (for lemon cake)

2 cups sour cream

DIRECTIONS:

1. Preheat the oven to 325 degrees. Butter and flour two 10-inch round cake pans.

2. Sift together the flour, baking powder, baking soda, and salt.

3. In another bowl, cream the butter and $4\frac{1}{2}$ cups of the sugar until light and fluffy.

4. Add the eggs, one at a time, beating well after each addition.

5. Stir in the vanilla. If you're making the lemon butter cake, add the lemon zest and juice.

6. Add the dry ingredients to the egg mixture, alternating with the sour cream.

7. Scrape the batter into the prepared cake pans.

8. Sprinkle the remaining $\frac{1}{2}$ cup sugar on top of the batter. Bake until set and a cake tester inserted in the center comes out clean (about 1 hour).

9. Let the cakes cool in their pans, then invert them onto a rack.

CHOCOLATE ALMOND TORTE

This is a moist, dense cake with a delicate chocolate flavor. I like to toast the almond flour to bring out the nutty flavor and add a subtle crunchy texture. If you are unable to find almond flour, you can make it yourself by chopping blanched, unsalted almonds in a food processor.

To toast almond flour, place it on a baking sheet lined with parchment and toast at 325 degrees until the edges are slightly brown (10 to 12 minutes).

Makes: Two 10-inch cakes, 12–15 servings

Tools: Two 10-inch round cake pans; double boiler; 3 mixing bowls; standing mixer; rubber spatula; cake tester; cooling rack

INGREDIENTS:

12 ounces semisweet chocolate, chopped

$1^1/_2$ cups (3 sticks) unsalted butter

$1^1/_8$ cups plus $^1/_3$ cup sugar

16 egg yolks

12 egg whites

3 cups almond flour, toasted if desired (see head note)

$^1/_3$ cup bread flour or all-purpose flour

2 tablespoons grated semisweet chocolate

$^1/_2$ teaspoon baking soda

$1^1/_4$ teaspoons salt

DIRECTIONS:

1. Preheat the oven to 325 degrees. Butter and flour two 10-inch round cake pans.

2. Melt the chopped chocolate in the top of a double boiler over gently simmering water.

3. Cream the butter with $^1/_3$ cup of the sugar.

4. Slowly add the yolks and beat well until incorporated.

5. In another bowl, combine the almond flour, bread flour, grated chocolate, and baking soda together. Set the dry ingredients aside.

6. In a third bowl, whip the egg whites with the salt until soft peaks form. Add the remaining $1^1/_8$ cups sugar and beat until glossy and firm peaks form.

7. Fold the melted chocolate into the egg yolk mixture.

8. Fold the chocolate egg yolk mixture into the meringue.

9. Fold the dry ingredients into the batter just until incorporated.

10. Pour the batter into the prepared pans and bake until set and a cake tester inserted in the center comes out clean (45–50 minutes).

11. Let the cakes cool in their pans, then invert them onto a rack.

ORANGE NUT CAKE

This cake is so rich, dense, and nutty that it can be eaten without any filling at all, but because of its intensity, I like to color the flavor with preserves, espresso, chocolate, or even a light splash of Sambuca. This recipe is a variation on one from Patisserie Lanciani in New York City. I have changed it a little, and added orange zest and a splash of rose-blossom water.

Makes: Two 10-inch cakes, 12–15 servings
Tools: Two 10-inch round cake pans; 3 mixing bowls; electric mixer; rubber spatula; cake tester; cooling rack

INGREDIENTS:

10 large eggs, separated

$2^2/3$ cups sugar

2 teaspoons rose-blossom water (optional)

1 tablespoon pure vanilla extract

Finely grated zest of 2 oranges

3 cups almond flour (see "Sources and Merchants," page 218)

3 cups hazelnut flour (see "Sources and Merchants," page 218)

$3/4$ cup heavy cream

2 teaspoons salt

2 cups frangipan (recipe follows)

DIRECTIONS:

1. Preheat the oven to 350 degrees. Butter and flour two 10-inch cake pans.
2. Beat the egg yolks with $2/3$ cup of the sugar until very thick and lemon colored, about 4 minutes. Add the rose water, vanilla, and orange zest.
3. Mix the almond and hazelnut flours and set aside.
4. Whip the heavy cream until it forms soft peaks and set aside in the refrigerator.
5. Whip the egg whites with the salt until soft peaks form, then gradually add the remaining 2 cups of sugar and whip until glossy and medium-firm peaks form.
6. Fold the meringue into the yolk mixture.
7. Fold in the whipped cream.
8. Fold in the orange zest and almond and hazelnut flours until incorporated.
9. Gently fold in the frangipan.
10. Pour the batter into the prepared cake pans and bake until set and a cake tester inserted in the center comes out clean (45–50 minutes).
11. Let the cakes cool in their pans, then invert them onto a rack.

Frangipan

Makes: 2 cups (1 pound)
Tools: Large mixing bowl; electric mixer; rubber spatula; lemon zester or cheese grater

INGREDIENTS:

7 ounces almond paste

$1/3$ cup sugar

6 tablespoons unsalted butter

1 teaspoon pure vanilla extract

1 tablespoon finely grated orange zest

$1/4$ teaspoon salt

2 large eggs

$1/3$ cup all-purpose flour

DIRECTIONS:

1. In a mixing bowl, combine the almond paste and sugar and beat until smooth.
2. Add the butter, vanilla, zest, and salt, and continue beating until incorporated.
3. Add the eggs one at a time, and beat until combined.
4. Add the flour and continue mixing until creamy. Store in an airtight container in the refrigerator for up to 4 weeks.

MIX-AND-MATCH FLAVOR COMBINATIONS

Here is a list of delicious layer cakes that can all be made with the following recipes:

Butter Cake layered with Chocolate Buttercream, sprinkled with chopped Candied Oranges and reconstituted dried cherries

Butter Cake layered with Praline Buttercream, chopped Candied Oranges, and a Grand Marnier Splash

Butter Cake layered with Semisweet Chocolate Ganache

Chocolate Almond Torte layered with Espresso Ganache and sprinkled with chopped reconstituted dried cherries

Chocolate Almond Torte filled with Praline Ganache

Chocolate Almond Torte layered with Vanilla Buttercream, sprinkled with chopped reconstituted cherries and a Grand Marnier Splash

Chocolate Blackout Cake layered with Espresso Buttercream

Chocolate Blackout Cake layered with Praline Ganache, with an Espresso Splash

Chocolate Blackout Cake with alternating layers of Praline Ganache and Vanilla Buttercream, and a Kirschwasser Splash

Chocolate Blackout Cake layered with Semisweet Chocolate Ganache and sprinkled with chopped Candied Oranges

Lemon Butter Cake (very thin layers) filled with raspberry preserves

Lemon Butter Cake filled with Vanilla Buttercream and thin layer of cherry butter (available at natural foods stores)

Lemon Butter Cake layered with Vanilla Buttercream with a Framboise Splash

Orange Nut Cake filled with Espresso Buttercream

Orange Nut Cake with a thin layer of raspberry preserves and Espresso Buttercream, with a Framboise Splash

Orange Nut Cake layered with Semisweet Chocolate Ganache

FLAVOR SPLASH

You can juice up a cake by splashing the layers with some extra flavor. It's easy. Mix a little of your favorite liqueur—Grand Marnier, Framboise, Kirschwasser, or even fresh-brewed espresso—with Simple Syrup (see recipe, opposite). A careful use of alcohol can add a whole new harmonic dimension to the flavor. Keep in mind that the layers will become soggy if you douse the layers with too much liquid. Also, alcohol content may vary between the different flavorings. You don't want your layers to be too strong or "hot" with alcohol, so be conservative with the splash, and be sure to taste it first.

SIMPLE SYRUP

INGREDIENTS:
1 cup sugar
1 cup water

DIRECTIONS:
In a saucepan, bring the sugar and water to a boil, then boil for 5 minutes. Remove from the heat and let cool.

Fillings

These are some fillings I use for my cakes. Not only are they delicious and easy to make, they also offer themselves to countless configurations with the aforementioned cakes. (See "Mix-and-Match Flavor Combinations," opposite page).

It is important to note that these fillings do not require immediate refrigeration. A cake filled with any of these can stay on a worktable in a reasonably cool kitchen for at least a day and a half. Once a cake has been covered with sugar paste and marzipan, it can no longer be refrigerated, because refrigeration will cause the icing to become sticky and sweaty.

VANILLA BUTTERCREAM

This silky-smooth buttercream has a light consistency, achieved by adding softened, creamed butter to a fluffy meringue. The stiff meringue also serves to fortify its structural integrity, making it easy to work with. Be aware that as you are making this recipe, the buttercream will go through a few stages, the first being the worst—it will appear broken and curdled and seem like a total failure. Don't worry, just keep on mixing it; it will come together and be creamy and perfect. It can be refrigerated for up to one week in an airtight container. At that time, remove it from the refrigerator, place it in a bowl on top of a double boiler, break up the cold pieces, warm up the buttercream without melting it down, and whip it back into shape with an electric mixer.

Makes: About 2 1/2 cups, enough to fill and
ice a 10-inch by 4-inch cake
Tools: 2 large mixing bowls; electric standing
mixer; whisk; saucepan

INGREDIENTS:
1 1/3 cups (2 sticks plus 5 tablespoons)
unsalted butter, at room temperature
1 tablespoon pure vanilla extract
3/4 cup sugar
3 large egg whites

DIRECTIONS:
1. In a mixing bowl, cream the unsalted butter. Add the vanilla.
2. In a separate bowl, whisk the sugar into the egg whites. Place on a pan of simmering water and heat only until the sugar is dissolved, whisking constantly to prevent the egg whites from cooking.
3. Beat the sugar and egg white mixture on high speed until it forms a medium firm meringue, about 5 minutes.
4. Reduce the speed, and add the creamed butter to the meringue, about 1/4 cup at a time. Continue mixing until the buttercream is smooth and creamy.

211

CHOCOLATE BUTTERCREAM

Add the chocolate ganache to the vanilla buttercream and there you have it.

Makes: Enough to flavor 2 1/2 cups of
    buttercream
Tools: Large mixing bowl; rubber spatula

INGREDIENTS:
1/2 cup soft semisweet chocolate ganache
    (recipe, opposite page)
2 cups vanilla buttercream (recipe, page 211)

DIRECTIONS:
Add the ganache to the buttercream.
Blend well.

MOCHA BUTTERCREAM

When mocha—the fine union of coffee with chocolate—is added to buttercream that has a touch of vanilla, you have mocha buttercream.

Makes: Enough to flavor 2 1/2 cups of
    buttercream
Tools: Large mixing bowl; rubber spatula

INGREDIENTS:
4 tablespoons espresso paste (see step 1
    of "Espresso Ganache," opposite page)
3/4 cup soft semisweet chocolate ganache
2 1/2 cups vanilla buttercream (recipe, page 211)

DIRECTIONS:
Add the espresso paste and the ganache
to the buttercream. Blend well.

PRALINE BUTTERCREAM

Add praline paste to vanilla buttercream, and you're all set.

Makes: Enough to flavor 2 cups of
    buttercream
Tools: Large mixing bowl; rubber spatula

INGREDIENTS:
1/2 cup praline paste
2 cups vanilla buttercream (recipe, page 211)

DIRECTIONS:
Add the praline paste to the buttercream.
Blend well.

SEMISWEET CHOCOLATE GANACHE

A deep, dark, creamy, and extremely versatile chocolate filling (or icing) which is delicious and very easy to make.

Makes: 3 cups, enough to fill and ice a
    10-inch by 4-inch cake
Tools: Medium saucepan; whisk

INGREDIENTS:
1 1/2 cups heavy cream
18 ounces semisweet chocolate, finely chopped

DIRECTIONS:
1. In a medium saucepan, bring the cream to a boil. Remove from the heat.
2. Add the chocolate and whisk until smooth. Ganache can be kept in an airtight container in the refrigerator for up to 2 weeks. Soften over low heat on top of a double boiler.

ESPRESSO GANACHE

This is a great way to cut some of the sweetness from a chocolate ganache. But the true character of the chocolate will still rise above the bittersweet espresso flavor.

Makes: Enough to flavor 3 cups of semisweet
    chocolate ganache
Tools: Small mixing bowl, whisk

INGREDIENTS:
4 tablespoons instant espresso granules
    (not freeze-dried)
2 tablespoons strong espresso (or strong coffee)
3 cups semisweet chocolate ganache

DIRECTIONS:
1. Add the espresso granules to the (liquid) espresso or coffee. Mix well until the granules are dissolved, making a thick paste (espresso paste).
2. Mix the espresso paste into soft ganache. Blend well.

PRALINE GANACHE

In the United States we equate the praline with those wonderful pecan sweets from the South. But in Italy, the praline is equated with hazelnut, a rich, flavorful nut with a high oil content, the best of which are grown in the Piemonte region, where it is called *nocciola*. To make things more confusing, American hazelnuts, which are mainly cultivated in the northwestern states, are called filbert nuts (named after St. Philbert, a fifth-century Gascon saint whose feast day is August 22, during the harvest). But no matter where it comes from, it all amounts to delicious nut butter. Whether it's called praline paste or filbert hazelnut butter, it can be purchased at specialty food stores, or by mail order (see "Sources and Merchants," page 218).

Makes: Enough to flavor 3 cups of semisweet
    chocolate ganache
Tools: Large mixing bowl; whisk

INGREDIENTS:
1/2 cup praline paste
2 cups semisweet chocolate ganache

DIRECTIONS:
Mix the praline paste into the soft ganache. Blend well.

TOOLS AND INGREDIENTS

Tools

I'm not big on gadgets. The following is a list of every tool I have used to make the cakes in this book. All of my decorations are made by hand because it's fun and challenging for me. However, there are a number of tools on the market that can make it easier for the nonexpert to create similar effects. Being a nonconventional traditionalist, I encourage you to challenge yourself, try it by hand, and if you're not satisfied with the results, then use the appropriate tool. If you can't find any of those locally, check the list of sources at the end of the book.

COOKING TOOLS

Candy thermometer: A heat-resistant glass thermometer used when cooking sugar.

Electric hand mixer: Good for whipping egg whites, egg yolks, cream, and other light ingredients.

Kitchen scale: For weighing ingredients. Available at kitchen supply stores.

Metal bench scraper: For keeping your work surface clean. Should always be by your side.

Metal spatulas: Small stainless-steel spatulas are useful for filling and icing very small cakes. Medium stainless-steel spatulas are useful for filling and icing medium to large cakes. Large stainless-steel spatulas are good for slipping underneath the cake tiers when you're ready to move them.

Paper towels: For cleanup and for helping pastillage bows to hold their shape.

Plastic bowl scraper: Like a rubber spatula, useful for scraping out bowls.

Rolling pins: Small, for rolling out pastillage and sugar paste decorations. Large, for rolling out large sheets of sugar paste and marzipan.

Rubber spatula: Essential to scraping down the sides of bowls of filling and icing.

Slotted spoon: A large spoon with holes in it for straining liquid from solids.

Standing mixer: This hard-working machine will fit on your kitchen counter. It's a worthy investment, and it will be with you forever. Good for heavier ingredients.

Turntable: Invaluable for cake decorating. Like a heavy-duty lazy Susan, it spins around with the cake on top of it, giving you access to all sides.

CUTTING AND SHAPING TOOLS

Cheese grater: For grating chocolate and zesting citrus peel.

Disposable penknives: The razor-sharp blade can be used instead of a paring knife.

Offset serrated knife: For cake sculpting.

Paring knife: A small sharp knife used for cutting small details in sugar.

Pruning shears: Heavy-duty cutters for cutting wooden dowels, available at hardware and garden-supply stores.

Scissors: For cutting parchment paper, trimming cardboard, and snipping the tips off paper cornetta.

Serrated knife: With long blade. For slicing cake layers.

Small pizza cutter: Great for cutting strips of fondant and gum paste.

CAKE-BUILDING TOOLS AND SUPPLIES

Cake drum: A heavy-duty base on which the cake rests. You can purchase premade pressboard or Masonite bases from a cake-decorating supplier or have them cut to order at a lumber store.

Cardboard cake bases: Disks that are placed under each cake layer. They must be in the same diameters as the actual cake layer: 8-inch, 10-inch, and so on. Available at cake-decorating suppliers.

Plastic dowels: Like architectural girders, these hollow plastic tubes can be cut to size to reinforce the structure of the cake. They are essential.

Separator plates: These round plates are made specifically for cake construction. They come in all diameters and are available at cake-decorating suppliers.

Wooden dowels: Wooden dowels can be cut to size and used to support cake tiers. Available at cake-decorating suppliers and hardware stores.

DECORATING TOOLS

Cornetta: A paper cornetta is easy to make and is used for doing intricate piping and detail work. It is like a miniature pastry bag, made from parchment paper.

Couplers: Two-part plastic couplers fit easily onto a pastry bag. They allow you to attach different decorator tips to the same pastry bag.

Decorating tips: There are hundreds of tips to choose from. However, I only use the following for my cakes: the #3, #4, #5, #6, and #7 round tips; the #18 (shell) tip; and the #47 and #48 basket-weave tips.

Gum-paste cutters: I use a petunia cutter for faux daisies and the flowers on Akbar's Cake. I also use the round open end of a cake decorating tip, as well as a few smaller-sized round cutters, which come in sets of five from 1-inch to 4-inch rounds. All are available at cake-decorating suppliers.

Gum-paste tools: These plastic tools are made to help you work with delicate gum-paste decorations. Available at cake-decorating suppliers.

Icing smoother: A plastic instrument for smoothing bumps and creases out of marzipan and sugar paste. Available at cake-decorating suppliers.

Large makeup brush: For dusting excess bits of sugar and icing from the cake.

Metal ruler: For measuring the height and width of cake tiers, as well as for measuring decorations. Also useful for drawing straight lines on cakes.

Paintbrushes: For painting and gilding. Sable brushes are more expensive but easier to work with. Available at art-supply and craft stores.

Palette: A plate for your colors.

Parchment paper: Along with its common use, which is to line baking pans, it's used for paper cones, practice surfaces, and tracing paper. Available in 18-by-24-inch sheets in large quantities, or in small rolls from baking suppliers.

Pastry bags: Lightweight polyurethane bags are easier to clean and work with. I like to use the #10, #12, and #14 sizes—no bigger.

Plastic wrap: For storing extra pastillage and sugar paste.

Tweezers: For lifting off excess crumbs that are hard to get at.

Ingredients

The following is a list of most of the edible ingredients used to make the cakes in this book. I have not listed some of the more obvious ingredients (butter, eggs, flour, sugar, milk, sour cream, lemons, and the like). As with the tools, anything you can't find locally should be available from the sources at the end of the book.

Almond paste: For making marzipan. Available in small quantities from the baking section of most supermarkets, or in large quantities from a baking supplier.

Cornstarch: Used to keep sugar paste and pastillage marzipan from sticking to your work surface and fingers.

Food coloring: Edible pigment for coloring icing and painting the cake. Found in a variety of colors and textures in cake-decorating stores and in primary colors at your local supermarket.

Glucose (or light corn syrup): An ingredient for sugar paste. Available at supermarkets and baking suppliers.

Glycerin: A lubricating ingredient for sugar paste. Available at cake-decorating suppliers and pharmacies.

Gold dust: An edible gold powder available only from cake-decorating suppliers. Mixed with lemon extract, it can be "gilded" onto cake decorations. Silver dust is available too.

Gold leaf: Real gold hammered into extra-fine sheets, which can be applied to the cake surface and to cake decorations. Available at art and gilding-supply stores. It must be 24 karat in order for it to be edible—do not use metal craft foil.

Gum tracaganth: A powdered vegetable gum that works as a catalyst when mixed into powdered sugar and water to make pastillage. Available at cake-decorating suppliers.

Lemon extract: Mixed into gold and pearl dust, it creates a liquid paste that can then be applied to the cake with a paintbrush.

Pearl dust: An edible shiny powder available from cake-decorating suppliers. Mixed with lemon extract, it can be "painted" onto cake decorations, creating an iridescent finish.

Piping gel: A clear sugar-based gel that can be mixed with spirits and applied to cake surface to create a glaze-like finish.

Powdered egg whites: A substitute for fresh egg whites. Available at cake-decorating suppliers.

SOURCES AND MERCHANTS

COOKING AND DECORATING SUPPLIES

American Bakels
Premade sugar paste, gum paste, and other cake-decorating ingredients
(800) 799-2253

Beryl's Cake Decorating Equipment
Large selection of cake-decorating supplies by mail order
P.O. Box 1584
North Springfield, VA 22151
(800) 488-2749 or
(703) 256-6951
Fax: (703) 750-3779
www.beryls.com

New York Cake and Baking Distributor
Large selection of cake-decorating supplies
56 West 22nd Street
New York, NY 10010
(212) 675-CAKE (675-2253)
(800) 94-CAKE-9 (942-2539)

New York Cake Supplies
Large selection of baking and cake decorating supplies available online.
www.nycakesupplies.com

Pfeil and Holing
Large selection of baking and cake-decorating supplies
(718) 545-4600 or
(800) 247-7955
Fax: (718) 932-7513
www.cakedeco.com

Wilton Enterprises
Makers of cake-decorating colors, decorating tips, and other cake-decorating supplies
2240 West 75th Street
Woodridge, IL 60517
(800) 942-8881
www.wilton.com

SPECIALTY FOODS

A.L. Bazzini Co.
Dried fruit, nut flours, almond paste, and premade marzipan
339 Greenwich Street
New York, NY 10013
(212) 334-1280

Dean & Deluca
Specialty food items, select kitchen equipment, and cookbooks
560 Broadway
New York, NY 10012
(212) 226-6800
www.dean-deluca.com

Dechoix Specialty Foods
Praline paste, chocolate, good-quality preserves, and other specialty food items
58-25 52nd Avenue
Woodside, NY 11377
(718) 507-8080
Fax: (718) 335-9150

KITCHEN EQUIPMENT

Bridge Kitchen Ware
Large selection of professional kitchenware
214 East 52nd Street
New York, NY 10022
(212) 688-4220
www.bridgekitchenware.com

Broadway Panhandler
Kitchen equipment for the serious home cook, basic cake-decorating supplies, and select cookbooks
477 Broome Street
New York, NY 10013
(212) 966-3434 or
(866) 266-5927
www.broadwaypanhandler.com

Williams-Sonoma
Kitchen equipment, select cookbooks, and cake-decorating tools for the home and professional kitchen
(800) 541-2233
www.williams-sonoma.com

SPECIALTY BOOKSTORES

Kitchen Arts and Letters
A bookstore passionately devoted to books on food and wine
1435 Lexington Avenue
New York, NY 10128
(212) 876-5550
www.kitchenartsandletters.com

Metropolitan Museum Bookstore
5th Avenue at 82nd Street
New York, NY 10028
(212) 535-7710
www.metmuseum.org

ART SUPPLIES

Pearl Paint
308 Canal Street
New York, NY 10013
(212) 431-7932
www.pearlpaint.com

BIBLIOGRAPHY

Barocco, Ambiente. *Life and the Arts in the Baroque Palaces in Rome.* New Haven: Yale University Press, 1999.

Bracon, Jose. *The Key to Gothic Art.* Minneapolis: Lerner Publications, 1990.

Cennini, Cennino D'Andrea. *The Craftsman's Handbook: The Italian "Il Libro Dell' Arte,"* trans. Daniel V. Thompson, Jr. New York: Dover Publications, 1960.

Charsley, Simon R. *Wedding Cakes and Cultural History.* New York: Routledge, Chapman, Hall, 1992.

Craven, Roy. *Indian Art: A Concise History.* New York: Thames and Hudson, 1997.

Eco, Umberto. *Art and Beauty in the Middle Ages.* New Haven: Yale University Press, 1986.

el-Khoury, Rudolphe. "Delectable Decoration: Taste and Spectacle in Jean François de Bastide's La petite maison." In Allen S. Weiss, ed., *Taste Nostalgia.* New York: Lusitania Press, 1997.

Hall, James. *Dictionary of Subjects and Symbols in Art.* New York: Harper & Row, 1979.

Hawthorne, Nathaniel. *The Scarlet Letter.* New York: Barnes & Noble, 1993.

Lurker, Manfred. *The Gods and Symbols of Ancient Egypt.* London: Thames and Hudson, 1980.

McGee, Harold. *On Food and Cooking: The Science and Lore of the Kitchen.* New York: Collier Books, 1988.

Mathews, Thomas F. *The Art of Byzantium.* London: Calmann and King, 1998.

Mintz, Sidney W. *Sweetness and Power: The Place of Sugar in Modern History.* New York: Penguin Books, 1985.

Peachey, Stuart. *Cooking Techniques and Equipment, 1580–1660, Vol. 2.* Bristol, England: Stuart Press, 1994.

Tannahill, Reay. *Food in History.* New York: Three Rivers Press, 1988.

Van Der Elst, Baron Joseph. *The Last Flowering of the Middle Ages.* New York: Doubleday, 1944.

Voltaire, François Maric Arouet de. "Goût." In Denis Diderot and Jean le Rond d'Alembert, *Encyclopédie ou dictionnaire raisonné des sciences, des arts et des métiers par une société des gens de lettres (1751–1777),* quoted in *Taste Nostalgia.*

Weiss, Allen S., ed., *Taste Nostalgia.* New York: Lusitania Press, 1997.

PHOTOGRAPHY CREDITS

All photographs in *Cakewalk* are by and copyright © Quentin Bacon unless otherwise noted below.

Page 63, paisley full page bleed: © Tina Rupp

66, row of ursulines: © Michael Grand

67, trio of ursulines: © Lenora Todaro

68 center: © Tina Rupp

71 bottom row, right: © Michael Grand

75 bottom row, right: © Michael Grand

76, cake on sugar mosaic: © Courtney Grant Winston

77 top row, center: © Michael Grand

77 bottom row, center: © Margaret Braun

83 top row, center; middle row, left and right; bottom row, center: © Michael Grand

100: © Michael Grand

103: © Michael Grand

121: © Michael Grand

150: © Tina Rupp

155: © Tina Rupp

157: © Tina Rupp

158: © Tina Rupp

159: © Margaret Braun;

174: © Tina Rupp

178: © Tina Rupp

181: © Tina Rupp

194: © Charles Maraia

195: © Tina Rupp

197: © Charles Maraia

217: © Tina Rupp

220: © Tina Rupp

ILLUSTRATIONS

The following artwork in food coloring and sugar is by and copyright © Margaret Braun.

Page 4: painting on pastillage; 7; 8: background; 9; 10: background; 12: background; 16; 27; 28: background; 37; 39: top, right; 40: background; 42: starburst; 46: background; 48–49; 56: center; 63; 64: top row, center; middle row, left and right; bottom row, center; 65; 71: top row, left; middle row, center; 75: fruit frame; 80; 82; 88: background; 91: background; 94–95; 97: background; 98: background; 102: background; 104–105; 107: background; 108: background; 112; 113: borders; 116; 118; 119: background; 120: background; 123 background; 124: background emblems; 127; 128; 130; 132: sugarwork molds; 136; 142: background emblem; 143: emblem; 144; background emblem; 146; 151: background; 159; 164–165; 166; 169; 170: emblem; 171; 172: emblem; 176–177; 179: emblems; 180; 186: emblems; 188: bottom, left; 190; 194; 195; 196; 206; 216.

INDEX

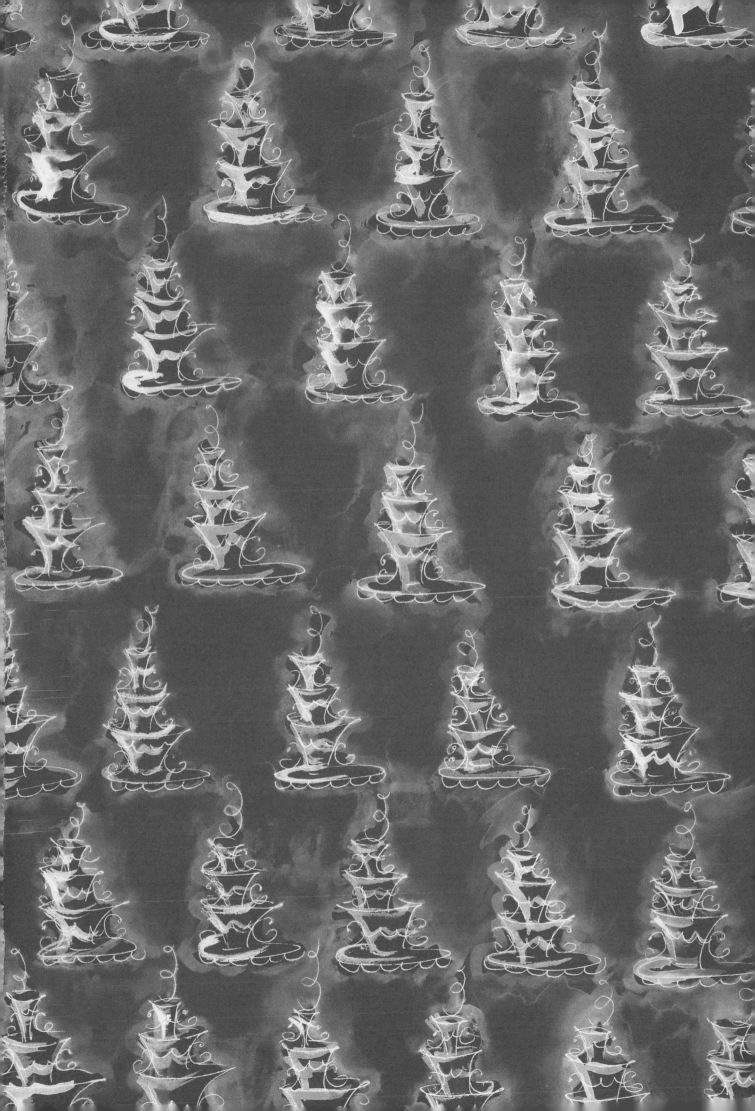

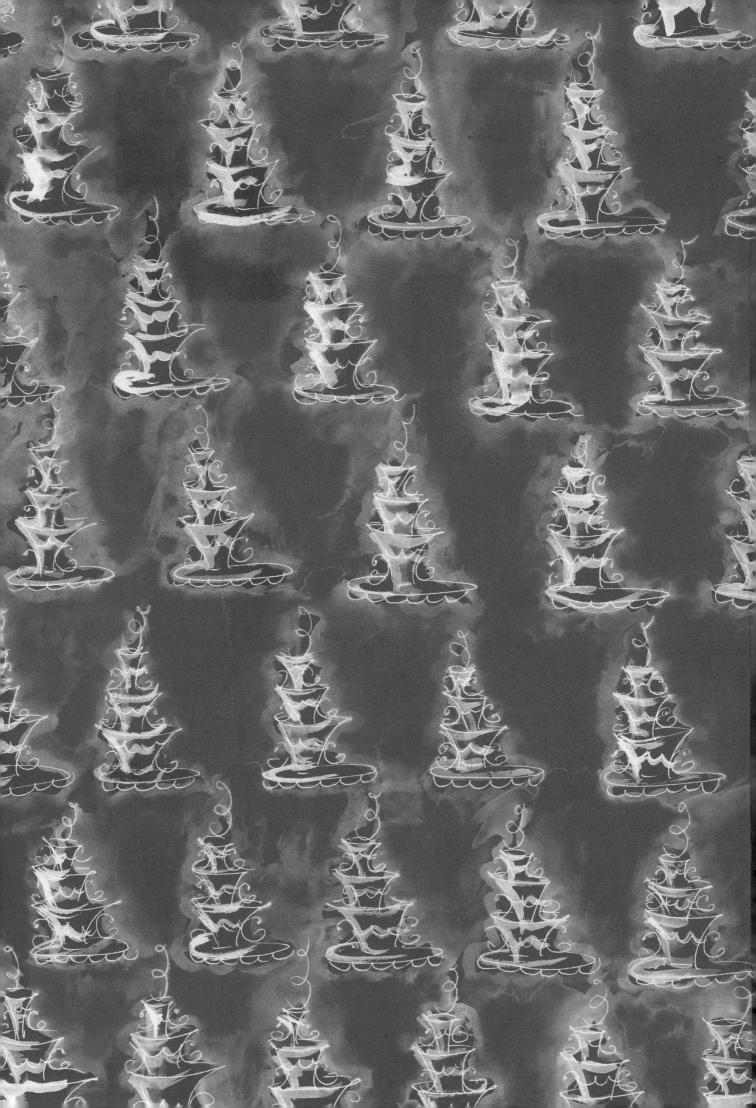